DELIGHTFUL BEADED EARRING DESIGNS

Written and Illustrated by

Jan Radford

Copyright © MCMXCIII by Eagle's View Publishing

All rights reserved. No part of this book may be reproduced or transmitted in any form or by any means, electronic or mechanical, including, but not restricted to, photocopying, recording, or using any information storage or retrieval system, without permission in writing from the publisher.

Eagle's View Publishing Company
6756 North Fork Road
Liberty, UT 84310

ISBN: 0-943604-37-0
Library of Congress Catalog Card Number: 93-70574

FIRST EDITION

DEDICATION

To my husband Jon, and our two daughters Jennifer and Susanne for their help and understanding of my dream and their help in making it all come true.

Radford, Jan, 1958-
  Delightful beaded earring designs / by Jan Radford --
  p. cm.
  ISBN 0-943604-37-0

1. Beadwork. 2. Earrings. 3. Jewelry making. I. Title

TT860   745.5942
                                     QB190-277

10 9 8 7 6 5 4 3 2 1

TABLE OF CONTENTS

About the Author	4
Acknowledgements	4
Introduction	5
Supplies	5
Bugle Bead Foundations	7
Single-Beaded Tops	7
Adding Thread	10
Removing Unwanted Beads	10
Double-Beaded Tops	21
Triple-Beaded Tops	25
Double-Beaded Seed Bead Foundations	29
Single-Beaded Tops	29
Double-Beaded Tops	35
Triple-Beaded Tops	43
Triple-Beaded Seed Bead Foundations	47
Single-Beaded and Triple-Beaded Tops	47
Loop Dangle Earrings	51
Miscellaneous Earring Styles	57
Single Seed Bead Foundations	57
American Flag	57
Eye	58
Triangular Post Earring	60
Earrings with Porcupine Quills or Long Bugle Beads	65

ABOUT THE AUTHOR

Jan has been designing and making beaded earrings for many years for her family and friends, and taking her designs to pow-wows, rendezvous, and craft festivals.

Jan was born in Houston, Missouri and now lives in Wichita, Kansas with her husband and their two daughters.

ACKNOWLEDGEMENTS

I truly wish to thank everyone who has helped me to fulfill my dream and worked at helping me to achieve it.

It is impossible to name everyone who has helped me, but to those of you who did, I wish to give you a very big Thank You. There is one very special person who helped more than anyone else - thanks Patricia.

INTRODUCTION

When learning to make beaded earrings, always remember that no one started out as an expert. It is a learning process that takes time and practice. Anyone willing to be patient and to try can learn to make beaded earrings.

The designs in this book can be made by anyone, from the novice to the expert, by following the instructions carefully. However, novices should probably begin with the more simple designs and work their way up to the more complicated designs. The novice who starts small can achieve many beautiful pieces and much satisfaction, while acquiring the skills needed for the larger, more complicated earrings. With a little hard work, these skills can be acquired in no time at all.

All of the earrings in this book are made using variations of the same technique, which is similar to the Brick or Comanche Stitch. The basic steps are described and illustrated in the first section, followed by a number of basic patterns. Everyone should read this section. Subsequent variations are briefly explained and followed by patterns featuring that variation. Please read the directions completely and make sure the entire procedure is understood before beginning an earring.

Before starting a project, always be sure to have all the necessary supplies on hand. There is nothing worse than being almost finished, only to break the last needle or run out of thread or beads.

Supplies

Beads: Seed and bugle beads are the most common beads used to make earrings. The size used is really a matter of personal preference. Size 11 seed beads are quite versatile and easy to obtain in many colors; they can be used with size 12 or size 10 seed beads, if a different size is called for in a pattern for effect or accent. No matter what size beads are used, sort through them and use those that are the most uniform in size and shape, so that the beadwork will look neat and the pattern will flow.

Bugle beads in sizes #2 (3/16"), #3 (5/16"), and #5 (3/8") can all be used with size 11 seed beads. Longer bugle beads can be used in the dangles, as can other larger beads which are available in a great variety of sizes and shapes. Beads, like yarn, come in dye lots, so be sure there are enough of each color (including discards) to complete the whole design before beginning to bead. Both seed and bugle beads are sold in strung bunches called hanks or loose by the ounce.

Thread: Be sure to use thread designed for beadwork. Nymo is a nylon thread made for just that purpose. Size B seems to work well with size 11 and 12 beads. Beeswax should be used to coat the thread. This helps prevent knots and tangles and also protects the thread from being cut by the sharp edges found on some beads.

Needles: Size 12 or 13 beading needles should be used. Regular sewing needles are too big to go through seed beads and forcing the needle through will break the beads.

Scissors: These should be a small sharp pair that have a good point for snipping close to the beads. Fingernail clippers also work quite well as long as they are sharp.

Pliers: A small flat-nosed pair work the best. They are used to help pull a stuck needle through a bead or to break unwanted beads.

Containers: Containers are needed to store beads by color, size and type. These do not need to be bought especially for the purpose. Any small jar with a tight fitting lid, such as small jelly jars or baby food jars will work. For long term storage, cases with drawers that can be seen through seem to work best, as they allow quick assessment of the beads on hand.

Findings: These are the materials such as earring wires (kidney wires, French hooks, etc.) and earring posts which are added to the beadwork to make wearable earrings. Although most of the patterns in this book include attachment loops for ear wires, these can be deleted and earring posts with pads glued to the back (top, center) of the earrings. Any craft glue made for these types of surfaces can be used (read the label).

Work Space: It is important to work in a place that is comfortable and has good light. The kitchen table works nicely.

BUGLE BEAD FOUNDATIONS WITH SINGLE-BEADED TOPS

Earrings made with a bugle bead foundation and with single seed beads in the top portion are the easiest to make, so they will be used to describe the basic technique used in this book. Before beginning to bead, choose an earring pattern from those which follow this section and use it as a guide throughout the construction process. One tip to keep in mind while beading: keep a steady tension on the thread and beads so that the beadwork will lay flat and have a neat, even appearance.

Step 1: The bottom section of the earring, consisting of the foundation and dangles, is beaded first. Begin by putting about 1 yard of waxed Nymo thread on a beading needle. Place one bugle bead (the first in the foundation row) on the thread (#1, Figure 1).

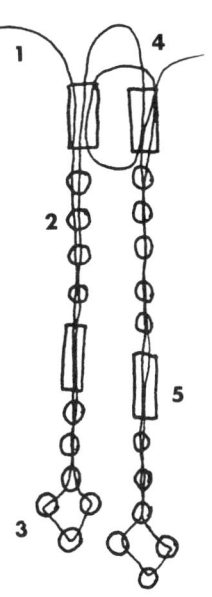

Figure 1

The loose end of the thread needs to be held tight, both to prevent beads from slipping off the end and to maintain the proper tension in the beadwork. Leave about three inches at the end of the thread and hold it between the thumb and index finger. A right-handed beader should use their left hand and a left handed beader should use their right hand.

Step 2: Put the first set of dangle beads on the needle and thread after the first bugle bead (#2, Figure 1).

Step 3: Determine which of the dangle beads will be used to form the bottom loop. This can be any number, from one to several, with three being quite common. Each pattern shows a suggested bottom loop, but this can be changed if desired. Bring the needle back up through all of the dangle beads except those chosen for the bottom loop (#3, Figure 1). Continue back up through the first bugle bead in the foundation row. Adjust the thread tension in the dangle so that the beads swing freely. The beads in the dangle should not be tight or bunched up, nor should there be thread showing between beads.

Step 4: String the second foundation row bugle bead on the thread. Run the needle back through the first bugle bead in the foundation row, from bottom to top. Then go through the second bugle bead again, from top to bottom (#4, Figure 1). Pull the bugle beads snugly together, but do not change the tension on the first dangle.

Step 5: String the beads for the second dangle and secure them with a bottom loop, in the same manner as the first dangle (#5, Figure 1).

Step 6: Continue in this manner, repeating steps #1 through #4, until the foundation row and all of the dangles are completed. Reinforce the foundation row and get rid of any gaps by weaving the thread back up and down through the bugle beads to the beginning of the row. The thread should come out of the top of the first bugle bead added to the row. Pull the beads snugly together, but not so tight that the beads bunch up or the thread is cut. At this point the loose thread end from the beginning of the earring may be woven through the foundation row beads and any excess cut off.

Step 7: The top portion of the earring is beaded next. Place a single seed bead on the thread. Run the needle under the thread loops between the first two bugle beads in the foundation row, from back to front. Then go back up through the seed bead just added (#7, Figure 2). The seed bead should lay flat on top of the bugle beads; the beads in the Figures are separated for illustrative

Figure 2

purposes only and in fact should be snug against one another.

Step 8: Continue in the same manner, adding single seed beads between each set of bugle beads in the foundation row. Work from left to right. There will be one less seed bead in this row than the number of bugle beads in the foundation row (#8, Figure 2).

Step 9: Add the second row of seed beads in the same manner as the first, but attach the beads to the thread loops between the seed beads in the row just added (#9, Figure 2) and work from right to left. Again, there will be one less bead in this row than in the previous row.

Step 10: Continue adding rows of seed beads to the top portion of the earring. Work back and forth until the final row, consisting of three beads is completed.

Step 11: String on six seed beads for the earring loop to which the ear wire will be attached. Take the needle under the thread loops between the first two seed beads in the top row, then go back through the six seed beads added for the attachment loop (Figure 3). Go from the first bead to the sixth and back through the six loop beads. Repeat this step 3 or 4 times until the loop feels sturdy (Figure 4).

Step 12: To finish the earring, weave the thread down through several rows of the earring top, then cut off any excess thread (see Figure 4).

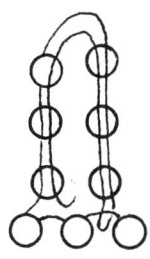

Figure 3

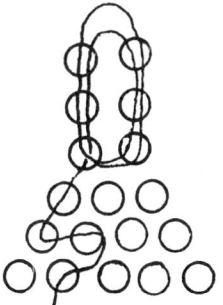

Figure 4

Adding Thread

If there is not enough thread to complete the earring, it is easy to add more without changing the appearance of the earring. When there are four or five inches of old thread left, weave this thread down through several beads in different rows to lock it in place. Cut off any excess. Take a length of new thread and weave it up through the beadwork to the place where the old thread ended. Be sure to go through several beads in different rows. Continue beading the earring as the pattern indicates.

Removing Unwanted Beads

If an unwanted bead is added to the thread, it is best to unstring the section and remove the offending bead. If this is not possible, then the bead can be broken to remove it, so long as it has not been sewn into the finished work. To break the bead, place the pliers on the flat sides of the bead, making sure that the thread is not between the jaws of the pliers (Figure 5). Apply pressure with the pliers until the bead breaks. Remember that beads are made from glass so take precautions against flying fragments. Do not place the thread or round edges of the bead between the pliers or the breaking glass of the bead will cut the thread.

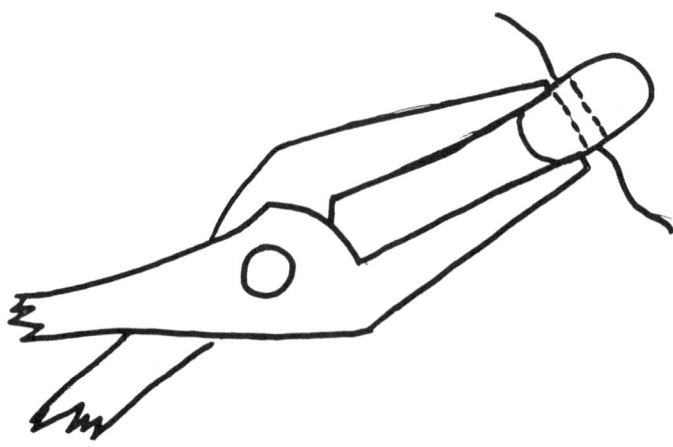

Figure 5

BUGLE BEAD FOUNDATIONS WITH SINGLE-BEADED TOPS

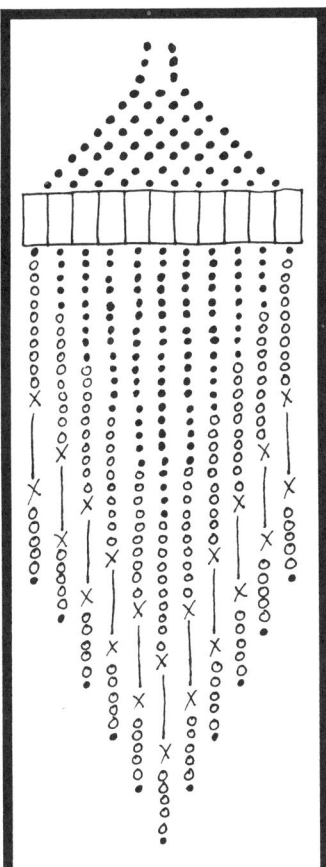

Pattern 1

- ▢ #3 Red Bugle
- │ #5 Red Bugle
- ● Silver
- ○ Trans Red
- X 3mm Silver Ball

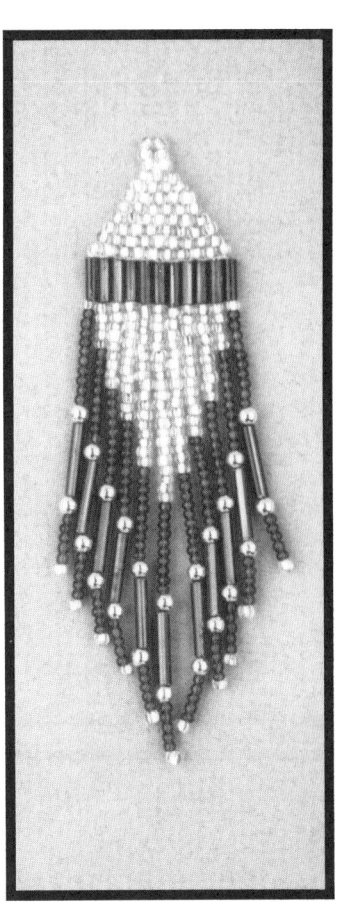

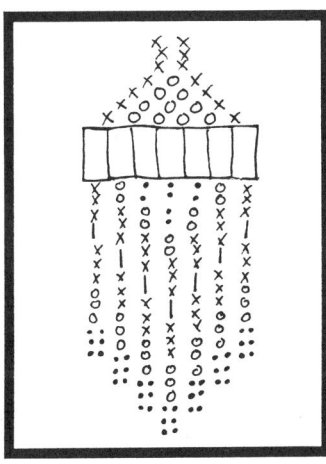

Pattern 2

- ▢ #3 Black Bugle
- │ #2 Black Bugle
- ● Lavender
- ○ Black
- X Pink

BUGLE BEAD FOUNDATIONS WITH SINGLE-BEADED TOPS

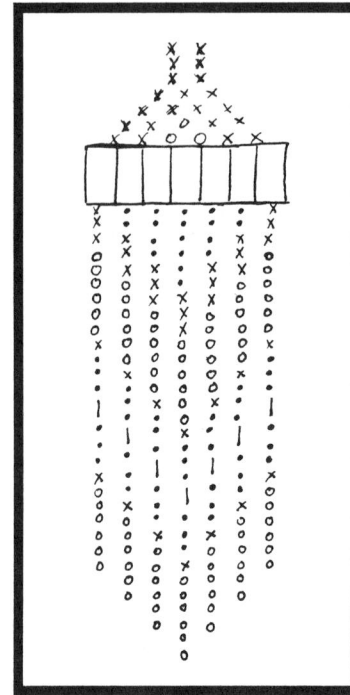

Pattern 3

□	#5 Black Bugle
	#2 Black Bugle
X	Black
●	Red
○	Blue

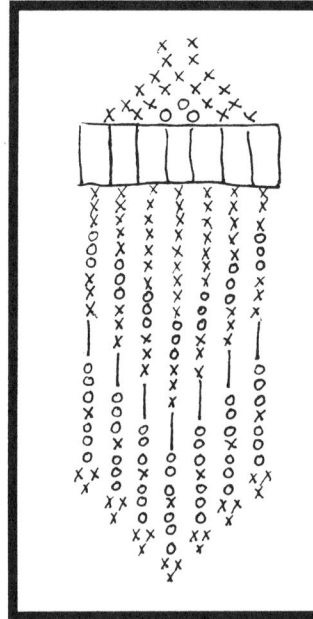

Pattern 4

□	#3 Silver Bugle
	#3 Silver Bugle
X	Silver
○	Black

BUGLE BEAD FOUNDATIONS WITH SINGLE-BEADED TOPS

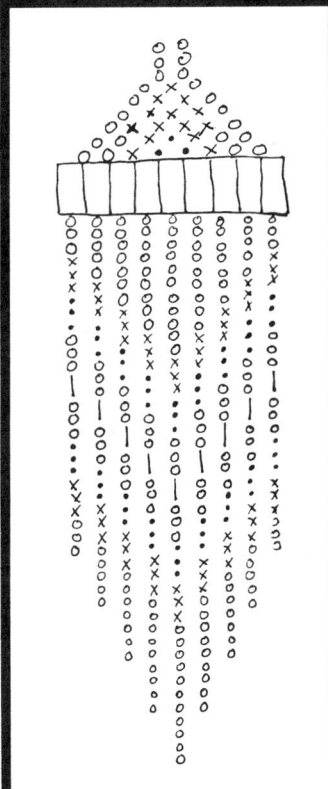

Pattern 5

- ☐ #3 Silver Bugle
- | #3 Silver Bugle
- X Red
- ○ Sky Blue
- ● Yellow

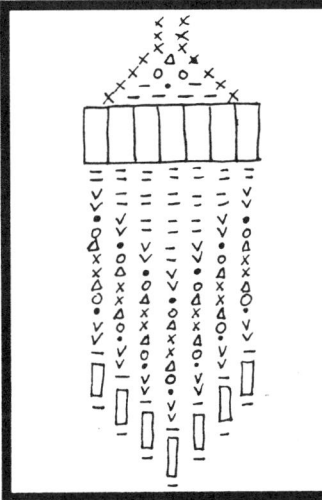

Pattern 6

- ☐ #3 Blue Bugle
- X Royal Blue
- — White
- ● Red
- ○ Orange
- △ Yellow
- V Black

BUGLE BEAD FOUNDATIONS WITH SINGLE-BEADED TOPS

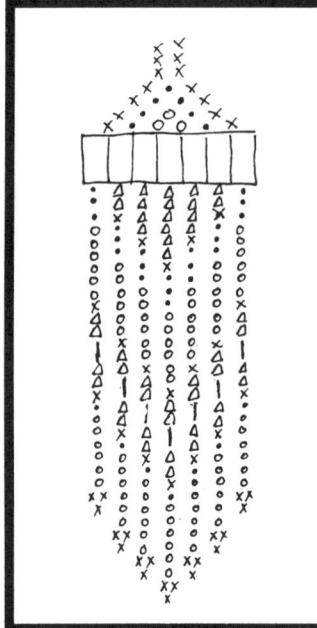

Pattern 7

□	#5 Black Bugle
	#2 Black Bugle
X	Black
●	Trans Red
○	Turquoise
△	White

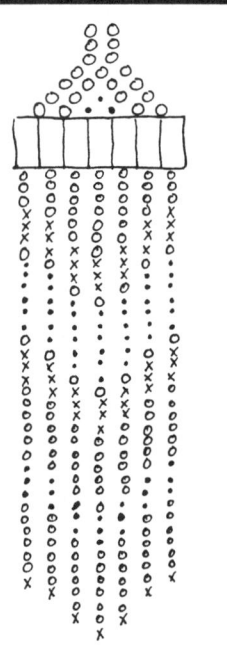

Pattern 8

□	#3 White Bugle
X	Lt. Blue
○	Trans Blue
●	Pink

BUGLE BEAD FOUNDATIONS WITH SINGLE-BEADED TOPS

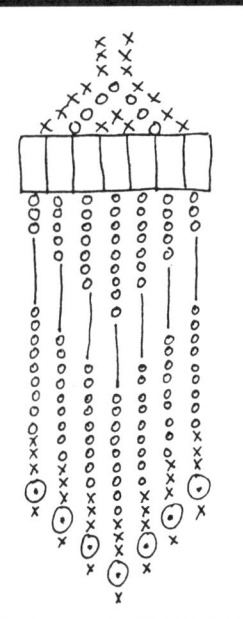

Pattern 9

- ▢ #5 Black Bugle
- | #5 Black Bugle
- X Black
- ⊙ 3mm Silver Ball
- ○ Silver

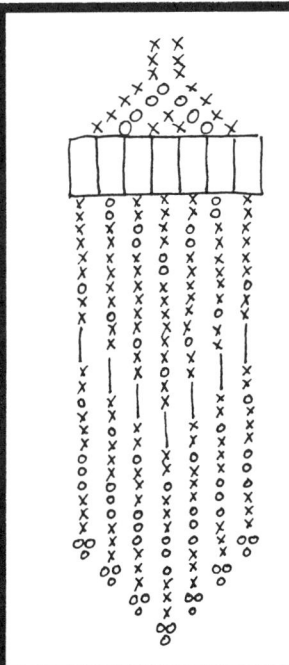

Pattern 10

- ▢ #3 White Bugle
- | #3 White Bugle
- X Red
- ○ White

BUGLE BEAD FOUNDATIONS WITH SINGLE-BEADED TOPS

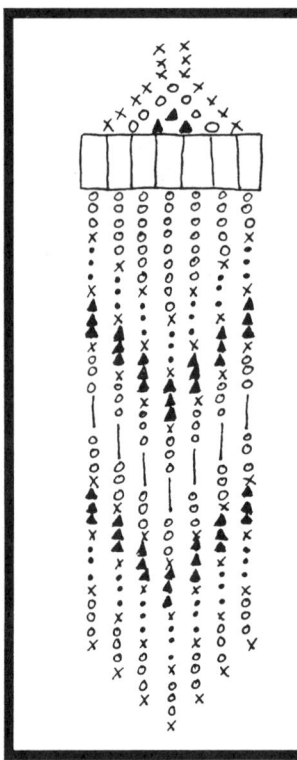

Pattern 11

- ▢ #3 Black Bugle
- | #3 Black Bugle
- X Black
- ○ Rasberry
- ● Pearl
- ▲ Pink

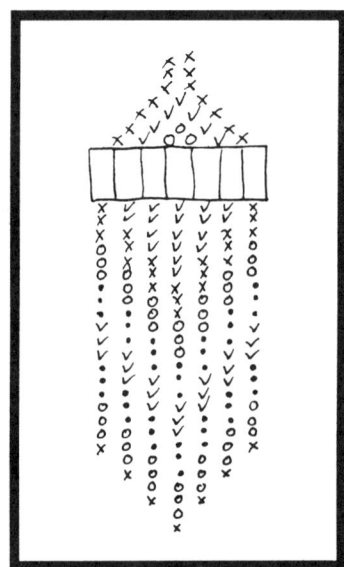

Pattern 12

- ▢ #5 Black Bugle
- X Black
- ○ Gray
- ● Silver
- V White

BUGLE BEAD FOUNDATIONS WITH SINGLE-BEADED TOPS

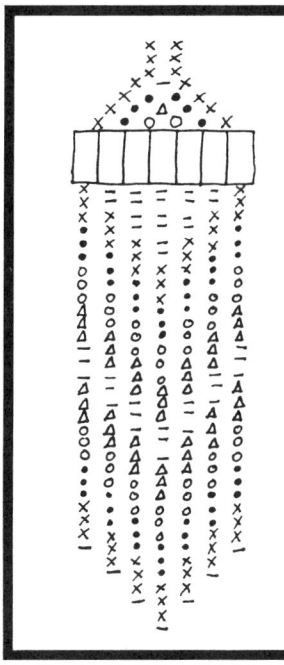

Pattern 13

☐ #5 Blue Bugle
X Royal Blue
● Red
○ Orange
△ Yellow
− White

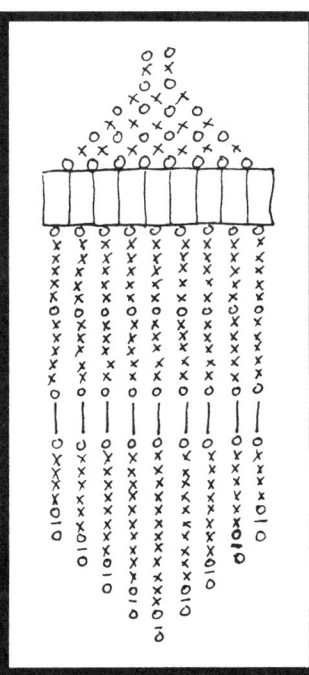

Pattern 14

☐ #3 Gold Bugle
| #3 Gold Bugle
X Silver
○ Black
− 3mm Silver Ball

BUGLE BEAD FOUNDATIONS WITH SINGLE-BEADED TOPS

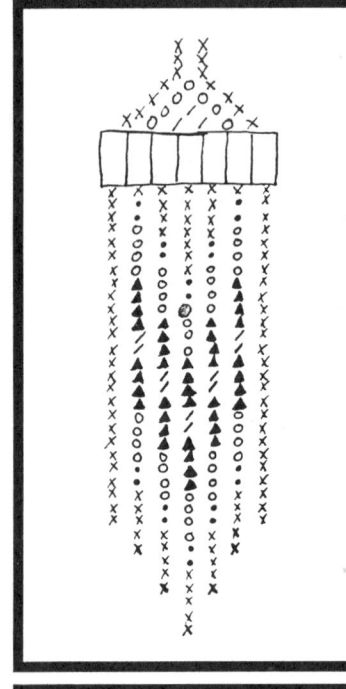

Pattern 15

- ☐ #3 White Bugle
- X Turquoise
- ● White
- ○ Yellow
- ▲ Orange
- / Red

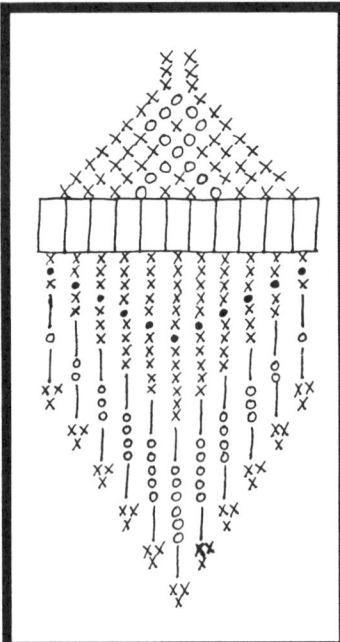

Pattern 16

- ☐ #3 Brown Bugle
- | #5 Brown Bugle
- X Rose Pink
- ○ Lavender
- ● Purple

BUGLE BEAD FOUNDATIONS WITH SINGLE-BEADED TOPS

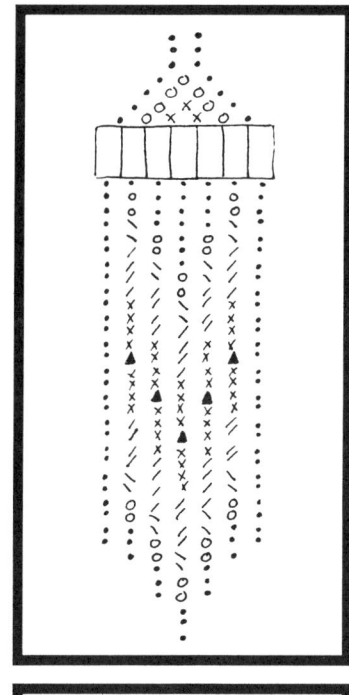

Pattern 17

- ▢ #3 Black Bugle
- X Black
- ● Turquoise
- \ Orange
- ▲ Trans Red
- ○ Yellow
- / Red

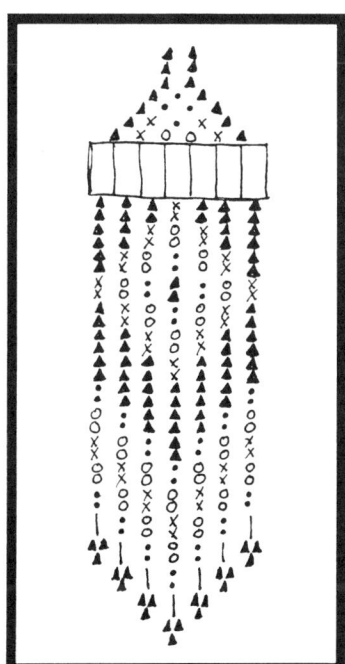

Pattern 18

- ▢ #3 Teal Bugle
- | #3 Teal Bugle
- X Red
- ○ Orange
- ● Yellow
- ▲ Turquoise

NOTES:

BUGLE BEAD FOUNDATIONS WITH DOUBLE-BEADED TOPS

This earring style is made in the same way as earrings with a bugle bead foundation and single beaded tops. The difference is that two seed beads are used in place of each of the single seed beads in the top portion of the earring.

Make the foundation row and dangles following steps 1 through 6 on pages 7-8. To make the top portion of the earring, follow steps 7 through 10 (pages 8-9), using two seed beads wherever a single seed bead is required. Use the two beads as if they were one; they will sit on top of one another and each row will be two beads high instead of one bead high (Figure 6). In this variation, it is especially important to use beads of uniform size, so that each row will lay neatly on top of the previous row. For the same reason, be sure to keep a steady tension on the thread throughout the beading process.

Add the earring loop as described in step 11, using eight beads instead of six. Finish the earrings as instructed in step 12 (page 9).

Figure 6

BUGLE BEAD FOUNDATIONS WITH DOUBLE-BEADED TOPS

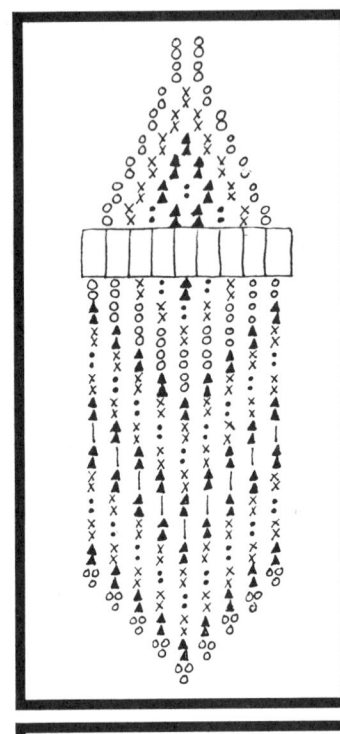

Pattern 19

- ☐ #3 Black Bugle
- | #2 Black Bugle
- ○ Red
- X Orange
- ● Yellow
- ▲ Turquoise

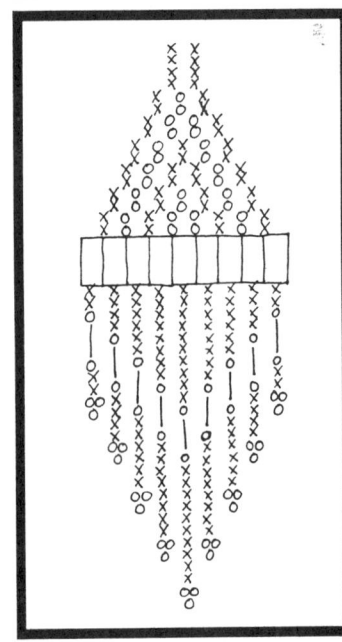

Pattern 20

- ☐ #3 Silver Bugle
- | #3 Silver Bugle
- X Silver
- ○ Black

BUGLE BEAD FOUNDATIONS WITH DOUBLE-BEADED TOPS

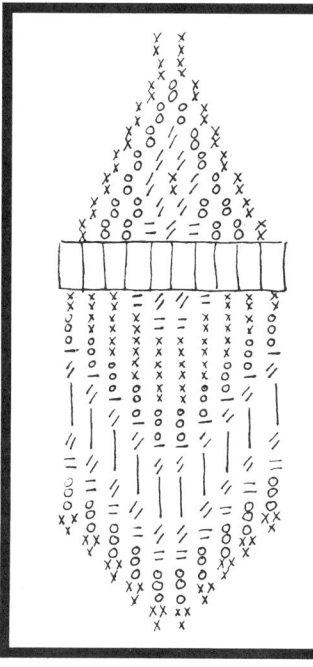

Pattern 21

☐ #3 Silver Bugle

| #5 Silver Bugle

X Turquoise
O Pink Pearl
— Gray
/ White

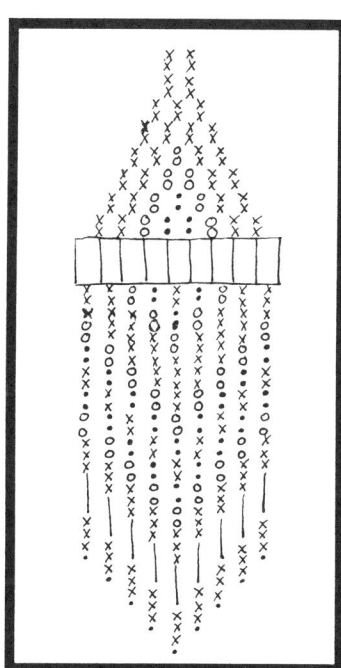

Pattern 22

☐ #5 Brown Bugle

| #5 Brown Bugle

X Ivory
O Tran Brown
● Rose Pink

NOTES:

BUGLE BEAD FOUNDATIONS WITH TRIPLE-BEADED TOPS

This earring style is made in the same way as earrings with a bugle bead foundation and single beaded tops. The difference is that three seed beads are used in place of each of the single seed beads in the top portion of the earring. Follow the patterns carefully as the three beads are not always the same color; also, in two of the patterns a 3 mm round bead is substituted for one set of three seed beads.

Make the foundation row and dangles following steps 1 through 6 on pages 7-8. To make the top portion of the earring, follow steps 7 through 10 (pages 8-9), using three seed beads wherever a single seed bead is required. Use the three beads as if they were one; they will sit on top of one another and each row will be three beads high instead of one bead high (Figure 7). In this variation, it is especially important to use beads of uniform size, so that each row will lay neatly on top of the previous row. For the same reason, be sure to keep a steady tension on the thread throughout the beading process; keep the beads flat and even, making sure they do not pucker.

Finish the earrings as described in steps 11 and 12 on page 9.

Figure 7

BUGLE BEAD FOUNDATIONS WITH TRIPLE-BEADED TOPS

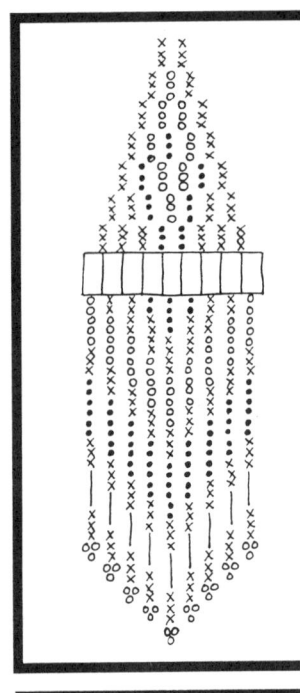

Pattern 23

- ☐ #3 Red Bugle
- | #5 Red Bugle
- X Trans Royal Blue
- ○ White
- ● Trans Red

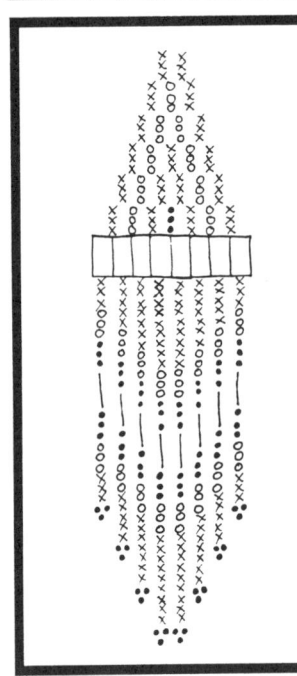

Pattern 24

- ☐ #3 Silver Bugle
- | #5 Silver Bugle
- X Silver
- ● Black
- ○ Trans Red

BUGLE BEAD FOUNDATIONS WITH TRIPLE-BEADED TOPS

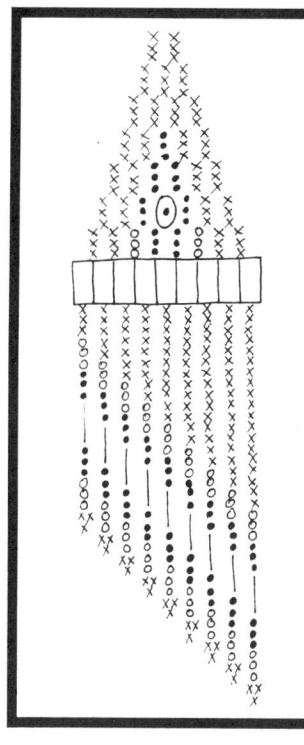

Pattern 25

- ☐ #3 Black Bugle
- | #5 Black Bugle
- X Crystal/lined Pink
- ○ Purple Iris
- ● Pearl
- ⊙ 3mm Silver Ball

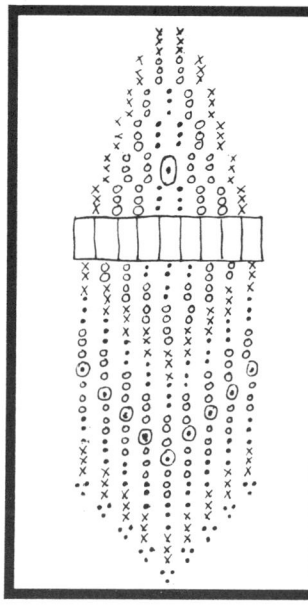

Pattern 26

- ☐ #5 Silver Bugle
- X Purple
- ○ Turquoise
- ● Pink
- ⊙ 3mm Silver Ball

BUGLE BEAD FOUNDATIONS WITH TRIPLE-BEADED TOPS

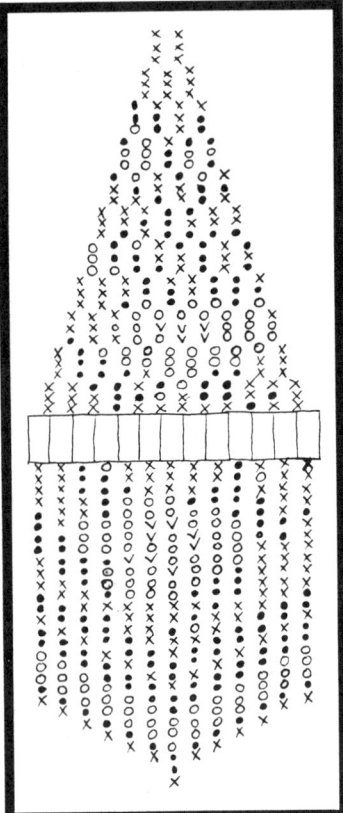

Pattern 27

	#3 Pearl Bugle
X	Pearl
●	Green
○	Red
V	Yellow

DOUBLE-BEADED SEED BEAD FOUNDATIONS WITH SINGLE-BEADED TOPS

In this earring style, two seed beads are used in place of the bugle beads in the foundation row.

To make the bottom of these earrings, follow steps 1 through 6 on pages 7-8, but substitute the two seed beads shown in each pattern for the foundation row bugle beads in the directions (Figure 8). Use the two beads as if they were a single bead; they will sit on top of one another and form a row which is two beads high.

Complete the earrings as describe in steps 7 through 12 on pages 8-9.

Figure 8

DOUBLE SEED BEAD FOUNDATIONS W/SINGLE BEAD TOPS

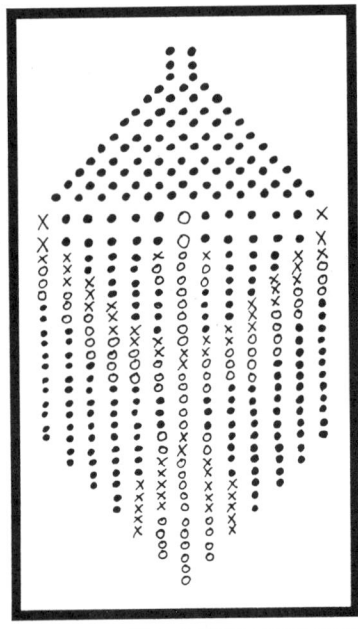

Pattern 28

X   Black
O   Brown
●   Blue

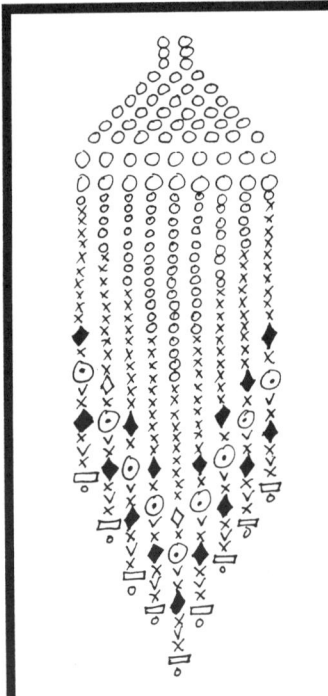

Pattern 29

X   Silver
O   Black
◆   3mm Black Facetted
⊙   3mm Silver Ball
V   2mm Silver Ball
▭   3mm Crystal Facetted

DOUBLE SEED BEAD FOUNDATIONS W/SINGLE BEAD TOPS

Pattern 30

- ▯ #3 Blue Bugle
- X Royal Blue
- ● Red
- ○ Orange
- △ Yellow
- — White
- V Black
- ⊙ 2mm Pearl Ball

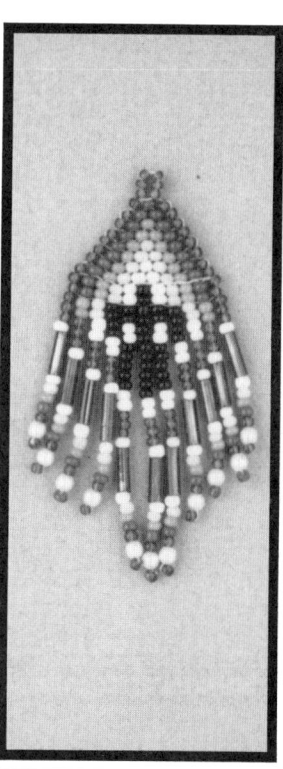

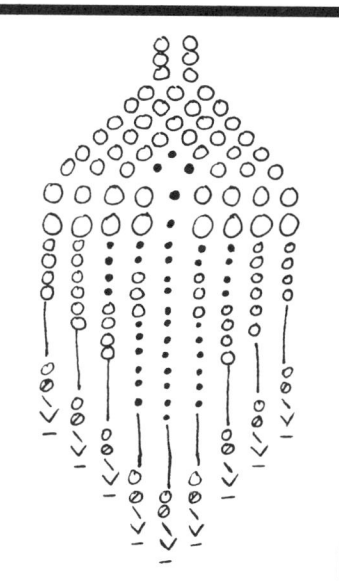

Pattern 31

- | #3 Red Bugle
- ○ Light Blue
- ● Royal Blue
- ⊘ Red
- V Yellow
- — White
- \ Orange

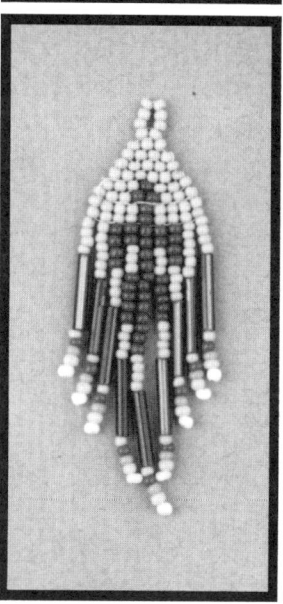

DOUBLE SEED BEAD FOUNDATIONS W/SINGLE BEAD TOPS

Pattern 32

| #2 Turq Bugle
X Trans Turquoise
○ White
▲ Yellow
● Orange
— Red
⊙ 2mm Pearl Ball

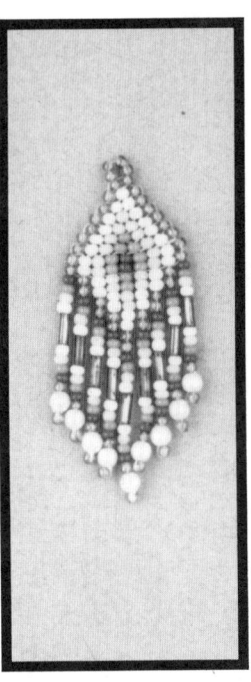

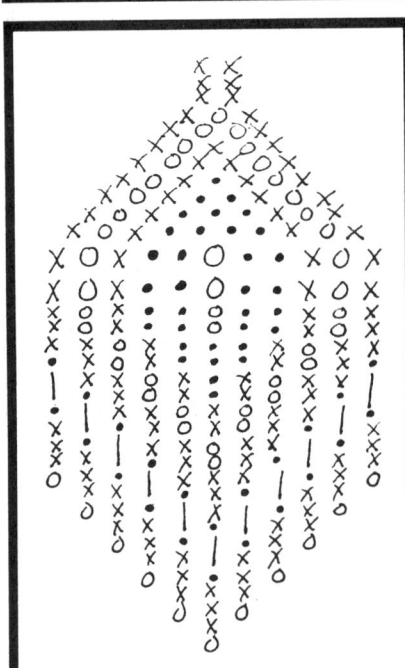

Pattern 33

| #3 Blue Bugle

X Light Blue
○ Dark Blue
● Crystal/lined White

DOUBLE SEED BEAD FOUNDATIONS W/SINGLE BEAD TOPS

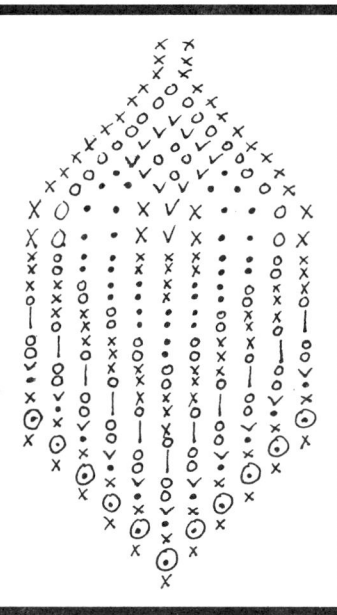

Pattern 34

| #2 Black Bugle
- **X** White
- ○ Black
- ● Red
- **V** Turquoise
- ⊙ 3mm Black Facetted

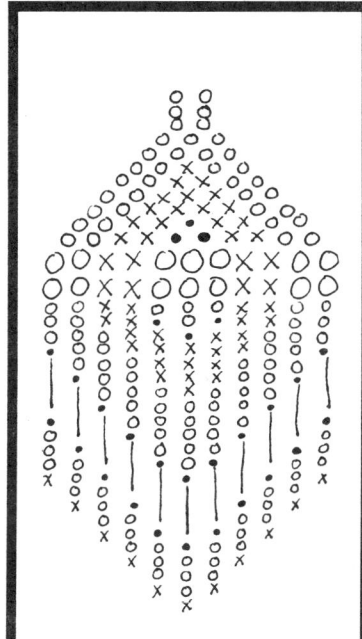

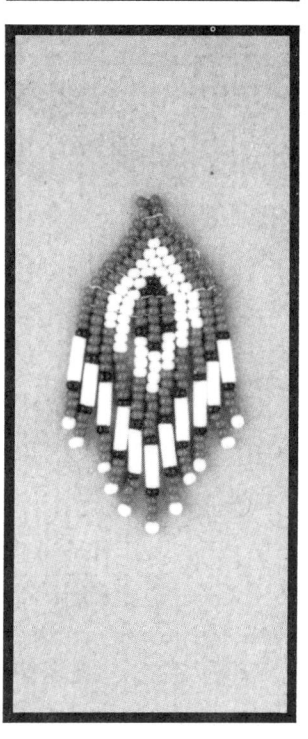

Pattern 35

| #3 White Bugle
- **X** White
- ○ Red
- ● Black

DOUBLE SEED BEAD FOUNDATIONS W/SINGLE BEAD TOPS

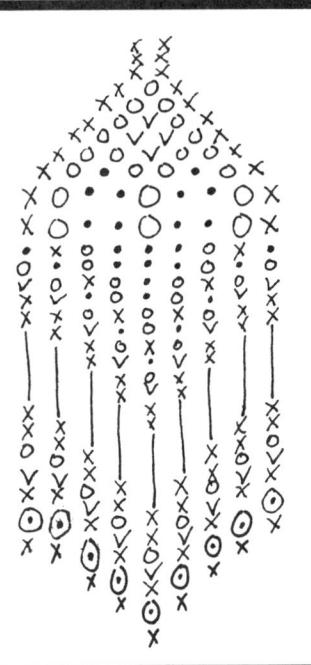

Pattern 36

| #5 Black Bugle

X Crystal/ lined White
O Trans Turquoise
● Black
V Crystal/ lined Pink
⊙ 3mm Black Facetted

Pattern 37

| #2 White Bugle

X Lt Blue Iris
O White
● Black
V Yellow
— Red
⊙ 3mm Blue Facetted

DOUBLE-BEADED SEED BEAD FOUNDATIONS WITH DOUBLE-BEADED TOPS

This earring style features two variations of the basic technique described in the first section. Two seed beads are used in place of the bugle beads in the foundation row *and* two seed beads are used in place of each single seed bead in the top portion of the earring.

To make the bottom of these earrings, follow steps 1 through 6 on pages 7-8, but substitute the two seed beads shown in each pattern for the foundation row bugle beads in the directions. Use the two beads as if they were a single bead; they will sit on top of one another and form a row which is two beads high (Figure 9).

To make the top portion of the earrings, follow steps 7 through 10 (pages 8-9), using two seed beads wherever a single seed bead is required (see Figure 9). Again, use the two beads as if they were one; each row in the top of the earring will also be two beads high.

In this variation, it is especially important to use beads of uniform size, so that each row will lay neatly on top of the previous row. For the same reason, be sure to keep a steady tension on the thread throughout the beading process.

Add the earring loop as described in step 11, using the number of beads shown in the chosen pattern. Finish the earrings as instructed in step 12 (see page 9).

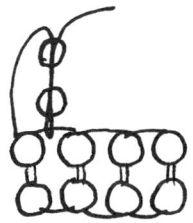

Figure 9

DOUBLE SEED BEAD FOUNDATIONS W/DOUBLE BEAD TOPS

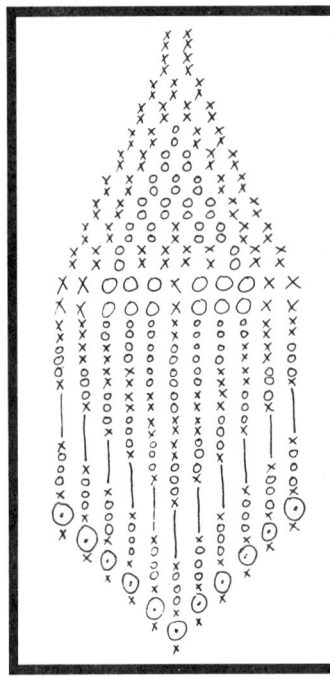

Pattern 38

| #3 Silver Bugle
X Black
○ Crystal/lined Silver
⊙ 3mm Silver Ball

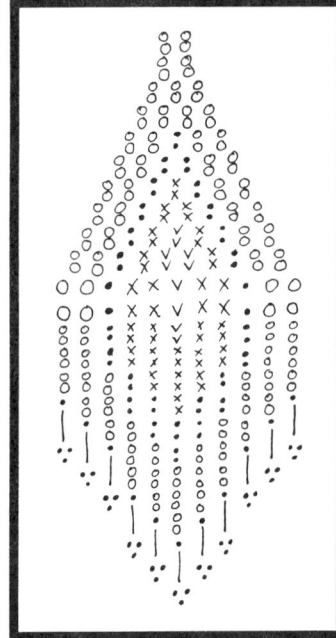

Pattern 39

| #3 White Bugle
X Lt Blue
○ Pink
● Dark Blue
V White

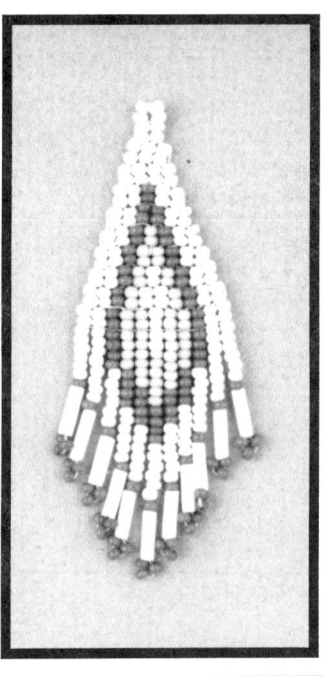

DOUBLE SEED BEAD FOUNDATIONS W/DOUBLE BEAD TOPS

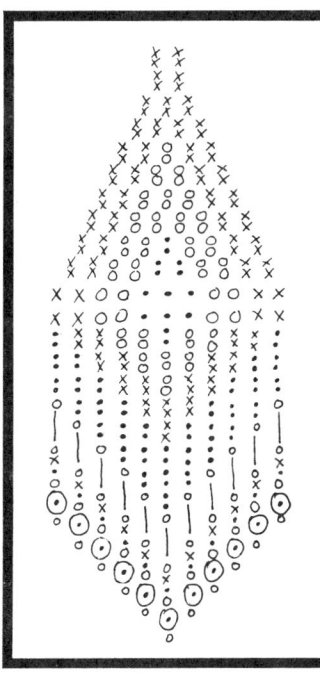

Pattern 40

| #2 Silver Bugle
X Turquoise
○ Black
● Red
⊙ 3mm Silver Ball

Pattern 41

| #2 Black Bugle
X Tran Purple
○ Crystal/lined Pink
V Black
⊙ 3mm Black Facetted

DOUBLE SEED BEAD FOUNDATIONS W/DOUBLE BEAD TOPS

Pattern 42

| #2 Black Bugle
X Tran Purple
● Tran Pink
V Black
○ Tran Blue
⊙ 3mm Black Facetted

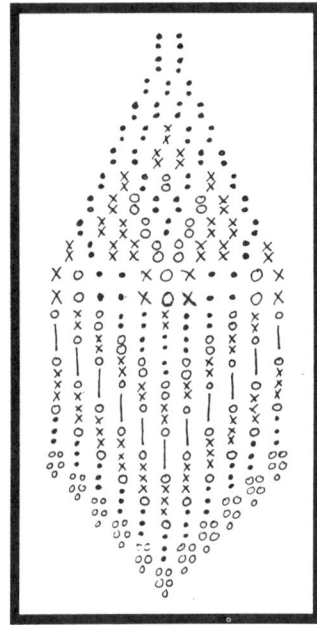

Pattern 43

| #5 Black Bugle
X White
○ Coral
● Turquoise

DOUBLE SEED BEAD FOUNDATIONS W/DOUBLE BEAD TOPS

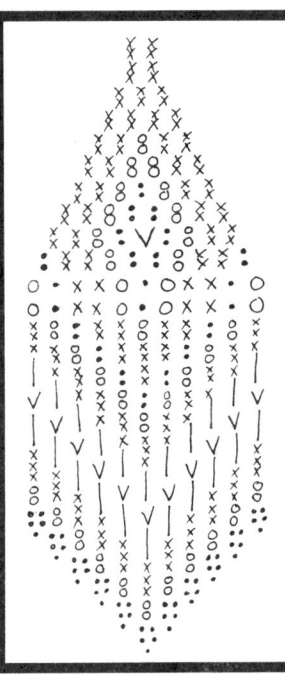

Pattern 44

| #3 Black Bugle
X   Trans Teal
●   Black
○   Purple
V   3mm Silver Ball

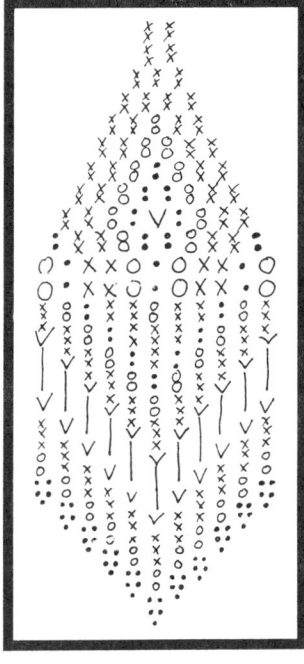

Pattern 45

| #5 Black Bugle
X   Trans Teal
○   Purple
●   Black
V   3mm Silver Ball

DOUBLE SEED BEAD FOUNDATIONS W/DOUBLE BEAD TOPS

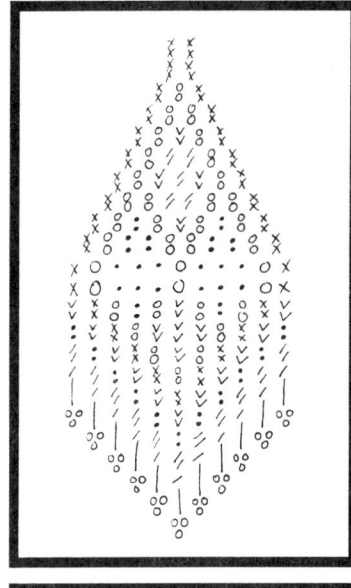

Pattern 46

| #3 White Bugle
X White
O Black
V Turquoise
● Crystal/lined Pink
/ Tran Purple

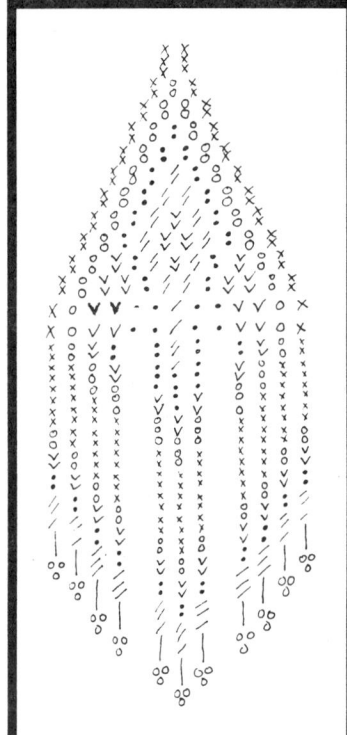

Pattern 47

| #3 White Bugle
X White
O Black
● Crystal/lined Pink
V Turquoise
/ Tran Purple

DOUBLE SEED BEAD FOUNDATIONS W/DOUBLE BEAD TOPS

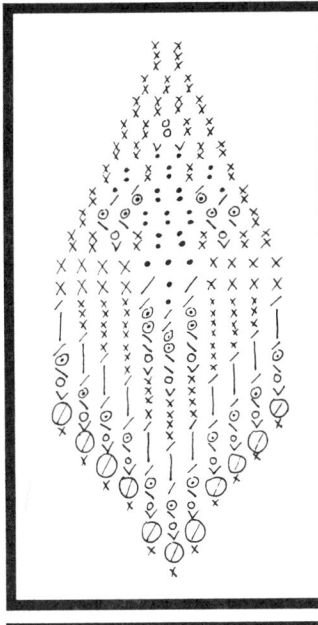

Pattern 48

| #5 Black Bugle

- X Turquoise
- ○ Orange
- ● Black
- ⊙ Red
- \ Light Red
- V Yellow
- / Brown
- ⊘ 3mm Black Facetted

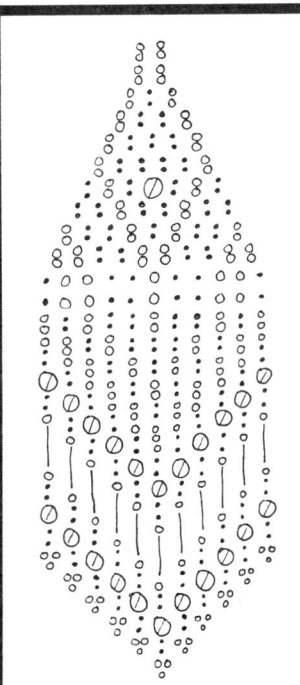

Pattern 49

| #5 Black Bugle

- ● Black
- ○ White
- ⊘ 3mm Silver Ball

41

DOUBLE SEED BEAD FOUNDATIONS W/DOUBLE BEAD TOPS

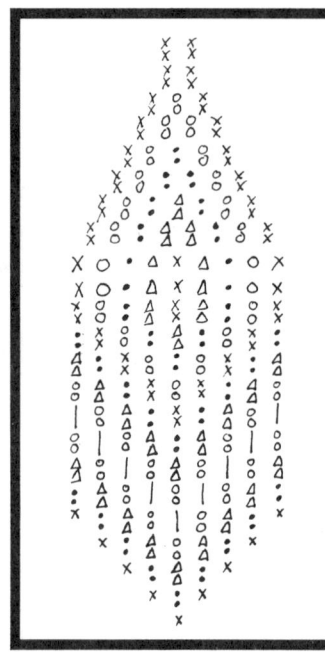

Pattern 50

| #2 Black Bugle
△ White
○ Red
● Turquoise
X Black

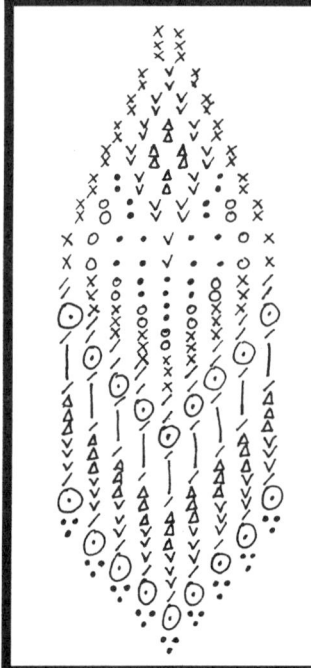

Pattern 51

| #3 White Bugle
X Crystal/lined Pink
○ White
● Yellow
V Coral
△ Green
/ Turquoise
⊙ 4mm Silver Ball

DOUBLE-BEADED SEED BEAD FOUNDATIONS WITH TRIPLE-BEADED TOPS

This earring style features two variations of the basic technique described in the first section. Two seed beads are used in place of the bugle beads in the foundation row *and* three seed beads are used in place of each single seed bead in the top portion of the earring. In one of the patterns, a 3 mm round ball is used in place of one of the sets of three beads in the top of the earring.

To make the bottom of these earrings, follow steps 1 through 6 on pages 7-8, but substitute the two seed beads shown in each pattern for the foundation row bugle beads in the directions. Use the two beads as if they were a single bead; they will sit on top of one another and form a row which is two beads high (Figure 10).

To make the top portion of the earrings, follow steps 7 through 10 (pages 8-9), using three seed beads wherever a single seed bead is required. Again, use the three beads as if they were one; each row in the top of the earring will be three beads high (see Figure 10).

In this variation, it is especially important to use beads of uniform size, so that each row will lay neatly on top of the previous row. For the same reason, be sure to keep a steady tension on the thread throughout the beading process and make sure the three bead sets in the top portion lay flat and do not pucker.

Finish the earrings as described in steps 11 and 12 on page 9.

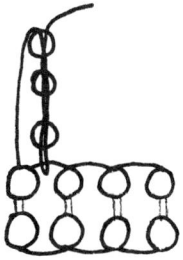

Figure 10

DOUBLE SEED BEAD FOUNDATIONS W/TRIPLE BEAD TOPS

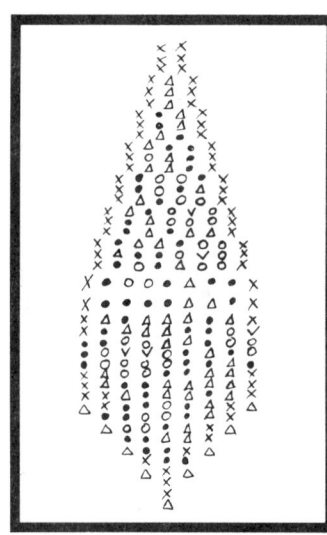

Pattern 52

- **X** Black
- ● Green
- ○ Crystal/lined Pink
- **V** Yellow
- △ Pearl

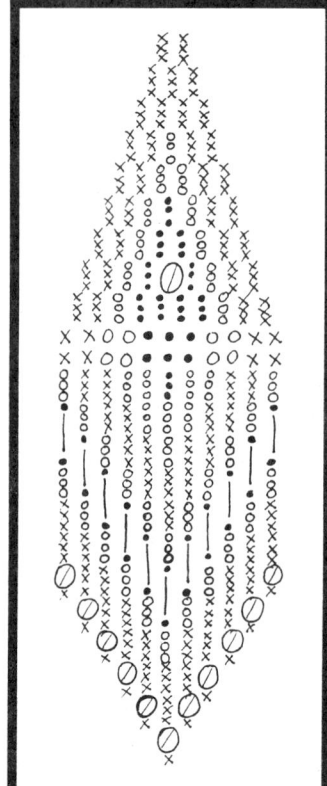

Pattern 53

- | 5/8" Black Bugle
- ● Red
- ○ White
- **X** Black
- ⊘ 3mm Silver Ball

DOUBLE SEED BEAD FOUNDATIONS W/TRIPLE BEAD TOPS

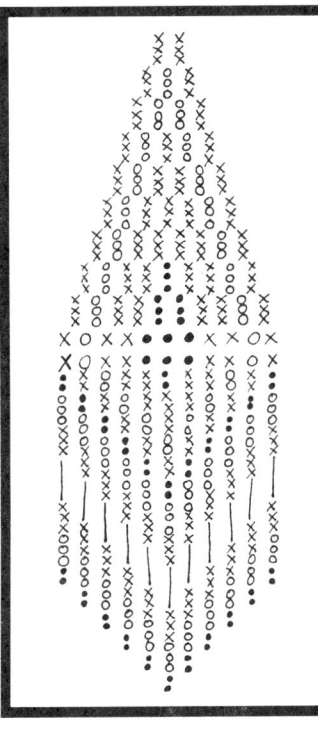

Pattern 54

| #5 Pink Bugle
● Pink
○ Crystal/ lined White
X Trans Royal Blue

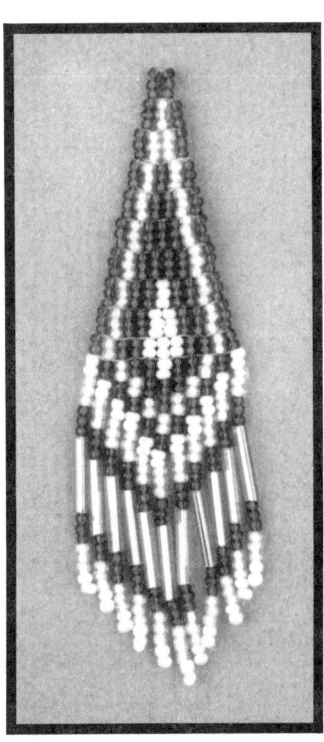

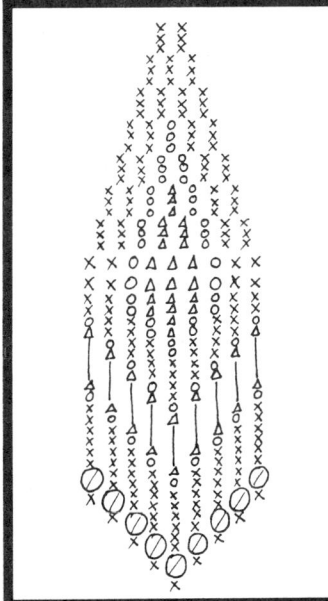

Pattern 55

| #5 Silver Bugle
X Black
○ Crystal/ lined Silver
△ Gun Metal
⌀ 3mm Silver Ball

DOUBLE SEED BEAD FOUNDATIONS W/TRIPLE BEAD TOPS

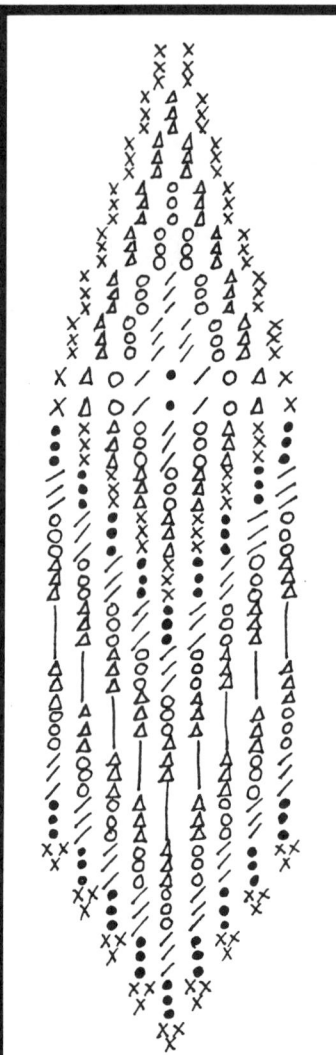

Pattern 56

| #5 Black Bugle
X Light Blue
● White
○ Orange
/ Black
△ Red

TRIPLE-BEADED SEED BEAD FOUNDATIONS WITH SINGLE-BEADED AND TRIPLE-BEADED TOPS

These earring styles feature two variations of the basic technique described in the first section. Three seed beads are used in place of the bugle beads in the foundation row. One of the patterns has a standard single-beaded top and two of the patterns use three seed beads instead of single seed beads in the top portion of the earring. It is also possible to use two seed beads in place of the single seed beads in the top portion of the earring, however no specific patterns for this are included.

To make the bottom of these earrings, follow steps 1 through 6 on pages 7-8, but substitute the three seed beads shown in each pattern for the foundation row bugle beads in the directions. Use the three beads as if they were a single bead; they will sit on top of one another and form a row which is three beads high.

To make the top portion of the earrings, follow steps 7 through 10 (pages 8-9), using either one or three seed beads (depending on the pattern) where a single seed bead is described. Again, if three seed beads are called for, use them as if they were one; in this case each row in the top of the earring will be three beads high.

In this variation, it is especially important to use beads of uniform size, so that each row will lay neatly on top of the previous row. For the same reason, remember to keep a steady tension on the thread throughout the beading process and where three bead sets are used, make sure they lay flat and do not pucker.

Finish the earrings as described in steps 11 and 12 on page 9.

TRIPLE SEED BEAD FOUNDATION W/SINGLE BEAD TOP

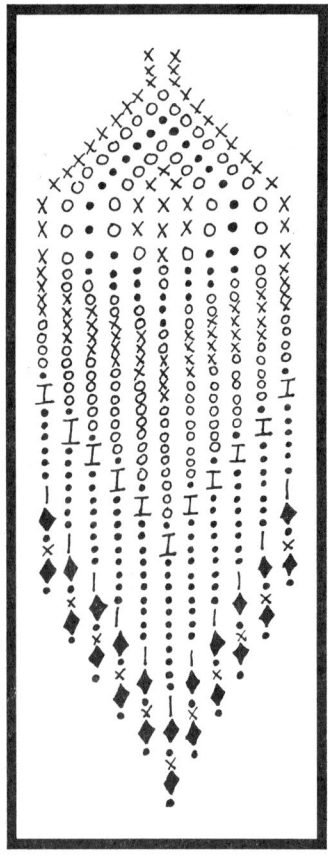

Pattern 57

| #3 Red Bugle
I #2 Blue Bugle
X Blue
○ Red
● Gold
◆ 3mm Red Facetted

TRIPLE SEED BEAD FOUNDATION W/TRIPLE BEAD TOP

Pattern 58

X	Purple
△	White
○	Orange
—	Black
●	Green
V	Yellow

49

TRIPLE SEED BEAD FOUNDATION W/TRIPLE BEAD TOP

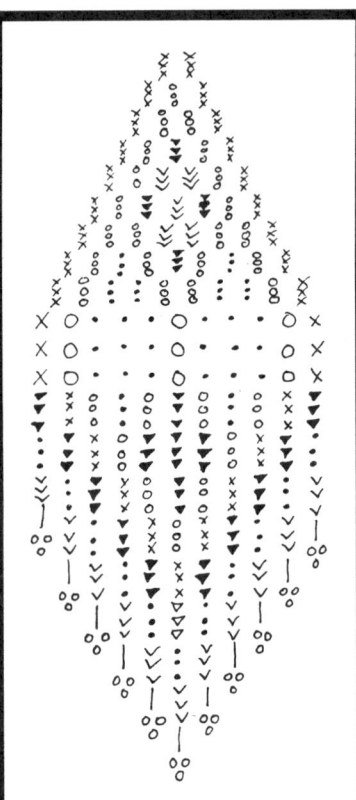

Pattern 59

| #3 White Bugle
X White
○ Black
● Pink Pearl
▼ Turquoise
V Purple

LOOP DANGLE EARRINGS

Loop dangles can be added to any of the earring patterns included in this book. Either a bugle bead or seed bead foundation can be used, and it does not matter whether the top portion of the earring is single-beaded, double-beaded or triple-beaded. The construction of the bottom portion of the earring requires a change in technique, however the basic instructions on pages 7-10 should be read before a pair of loop dangle earrings is made.

Step 1: For loop dangle earrings, the foundation row must be constructed before any of the dangles are added. String the first bugle bead or set of seed beads for the foundation row on the thread, then add the second bead or set of beads. Go back up through the first bead or set of beads from the bottom to the top. Tighten the thread, pulling the two beads (or sets of beads) snugly parallel to one another. Go down through the second bead(s), from top to bottom, and string on the third foundation row bead or set of beads. Attach this bead or set of beads to the foundation row by going up through the second bead(s) and back down through the new bead(s). Continue adding beads or sets of beads in the same manner (Figure 11) until the foundation row is complete.

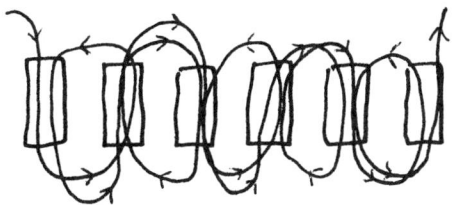

Figure 11

Step 2: The loop dangles can now be added. Rotate the beads so that the thread is coming out of the bottom, left of the foundation row. Using the pattern as a guide, string on the beads for the outside loop dangle. Take the needle up through the foundation bead(s) on the opposite end of the row and then down through the foundation bead(s) adjacent to the end bead(s). Adjust the tension in the first loop, then string on the beads for the second loop dangle. Take the thread up through the second foundation bead(s) from the left (Figure 12). Continue in this manner, working from the outside to the center of the foundation row, until all of the dangles have been added.

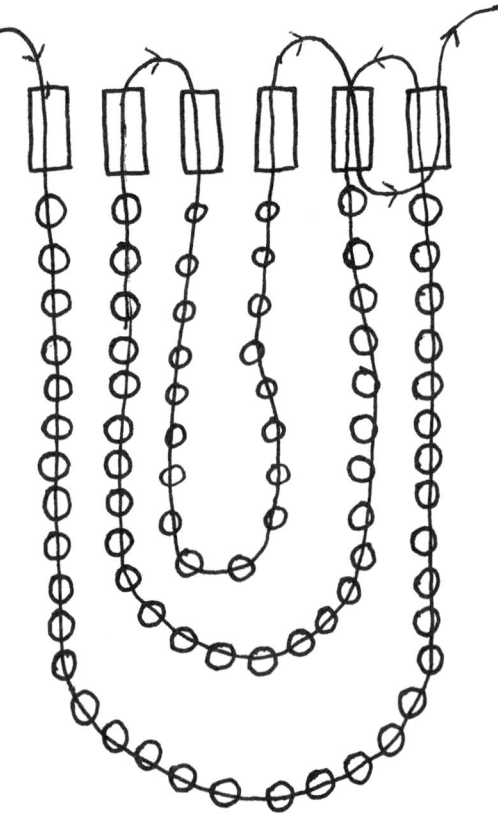

Figure 12

Step 3: Weave the thread through the foundation row beads to the right, so that the thread is coming out of the top of the end bead(s). To make the top portion of the earring, turn the beadwork so that the thread is on the left and follow steps 7 through 10 on pages 8-9. If the pattern is for a double or triple-beaded top, use two or three seed beads wherever a single seed bead is called for in the instructions [see Figure 6 (page 21) and Figure 7 (page 25)]. Finish the earrings as described in steps 11 and 12 on page 9.

BUGLE BEAD FOUNDATIONS WITH LOOP DANGLES

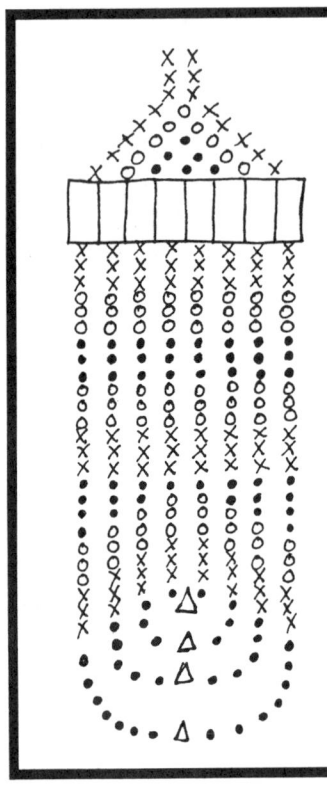

Pattern 60

- ☐ #3 Silver Bugle
- X Light Blue
- ○ Silver
- ● Black
- △ 3mm Silver Ball

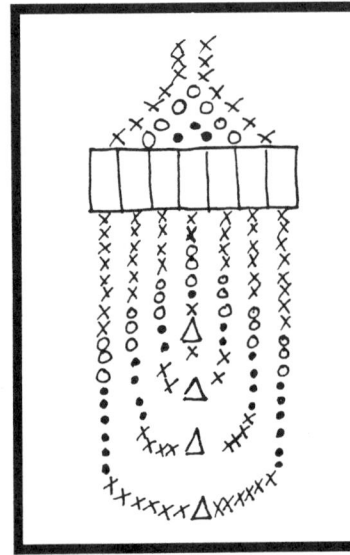

Pattern 61

- ☐ #3 Black Bugle
- X White
- ● Red
- ○ Black
- △ 3mm Black Facetted

BUGLE BEAD FOUNDATIONS WITH LOOP DANGLES

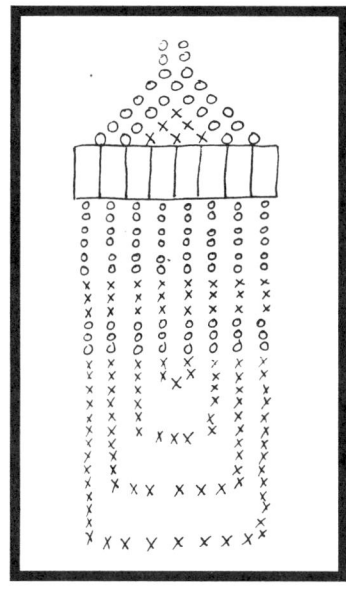

Pattern 62

☐ #2 Red Bugle
○ Red
X Ivory

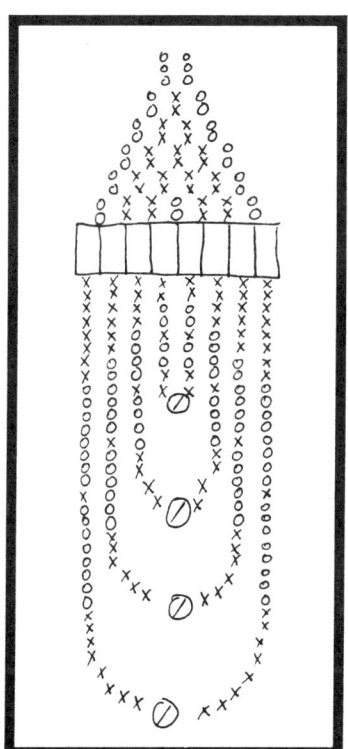

Pattern 63

☐ #3 Silver Bugle
X Black
○ Silver
⊘ 3mm Silver Ball

TRIPLE SEED BEAD FOUNDATION WITH LOOP DANGLES

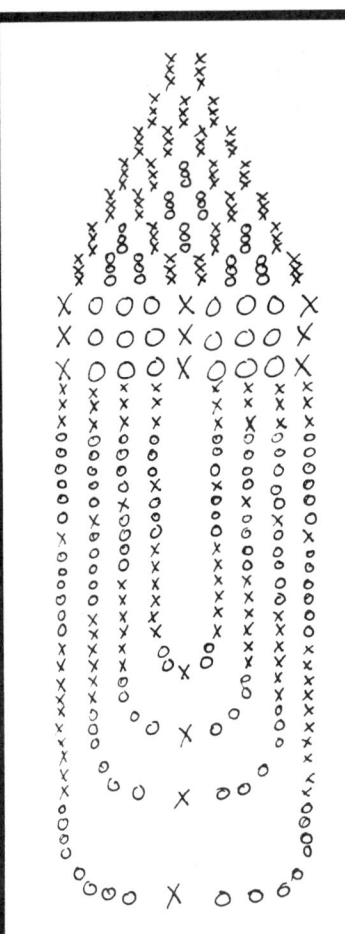

Pattern 64

X Black
O Turquoise

MISCELLANEOUS EARRING STYLES

Single Seed Bead Foundations

This earring style (Patterns 65-67) is also a variation of the basic technique described in the first section. One seed bead is used in place of each bugle bead in the foundation row, while single seed beads are again used in the top portion of the earring. The Santa and elf patterns are sure to gather compliments at holiday parties and they make great gifts!

To make the bottom of these earrings, follow steps 1 through 6 on pages 7-8, substituting the single seed beads shown in each pattern for the foundation row bugle beads in the directions.

To make the top portion of the earrings, follow steps 7 through 10 (pages 8-9). Finish the earrings as described in steps 11 and 12 on page 9.

American Flag Earrings

These patterns (68-69) have no top portion; the foundation is a section, rather than a row and is made in a different manner than any of the previous earrings. However, many of the concepts found in the directions on pages 7-9 will still be useful, and these instructions should be read before constructing this earring. This earring style is very popular!

Step 1: String the first vertical row of beads, including the beads in the foundation section *and* the beads in the first dangle. Leave a three or four inch tail on the loose end of the thread. Use the last bead as the bottom loop and go back up through the rest of the beads in this row (#1 in Figure 13).

Step 2: String the first two beads in the second vertical row. Then run the needle up through the first two beads in the first row. Bring the needle back down through the two beads just added (#2 in Figure 13) and string the next two beads in the second vertical row.

Step 3: Attach the second set of foundation beads in the second row to the third and fourth beads in the first row, using the same technique as was used for the first set. In the same manner, attach the third set of foundation beads to the fifth and sixth beads in the first row (#3 in Figure 13).

Step 4: String the rest of the beads in the second vertical row (the dangle beads) on the thread. Use the last bead as the bottom loop of the dangle and go back up through the beads to the top of the row (#4 in Figure 13).

Step 5: Continue adding vertical rows of beads, repeating steps 2 through 4 until the body of the earring is completed. To add the ear wire attachment loop, weave the thread over to the middle three beads at the top of the foundation section and add the loop as in step 11 on page 9. Finish the earrings as described in step 12 (page 9).

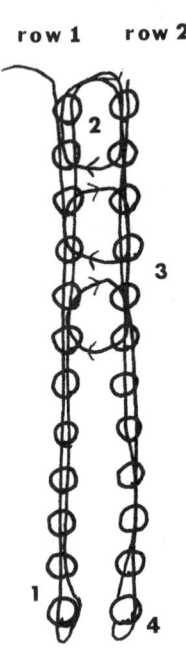

Figure 13

Eye Earrings

The technique used to make this earring (Pattern 70) is similar to that used to make the flag earrings, the difference being that the eye earring is begun in the middle. It is difficult to add thread in the middle of this earring, so be sure to start with enough thread for the entire earring (at least 24 inches).

Step 1: String the beads for the middle (longest) vertical row of the earring, including the beads in the foundation section *and* the beads in the first dangle. Leave a three or four inch tail on the loose end of the thread. Use the last five beads for the bottom loop and go back up through the rest of the beads in this row (#1 in Figure 14).

Step 2: String the first two beads in the vertical row to the right of the first (middle) row. Run the needle up through the first two beads in the middle row, then bring the thread back down through the two beads just added (#2 in Figure 14). String the next two beads for the second row and attach them to the third and fourth beads in the middle row, using the same technique as was used for the first two beads. Attach the third set of beads in the second row to the 2mm round ball in the middle row (#3 in Figure 14), then attach the fourth set of two beads to the sixth and seventh beads in the middle row. Attach the fifth set of two beads to the eighth and ninth beads in the middle row.

Step 3: String the rest of the beads in the second vertical row (the dangle beads) on the thread. Use the last five beads for the bottom loop of the dangle and go back up through the remaining beads, exiting between the first and second beads of this second row (#4, Figure 14). String on the first two beads of the third vertical row and attach them to the second and third beads of the second row. Attach six more foundation beads in the third row using the same technique as in the second row (there are a total of 8 foundation beads in this row). String the dangle beads for the third row, make a five bead loop at the bottom and come back up through the remaining beads, again exiting between the first and second beads in this row. Add the

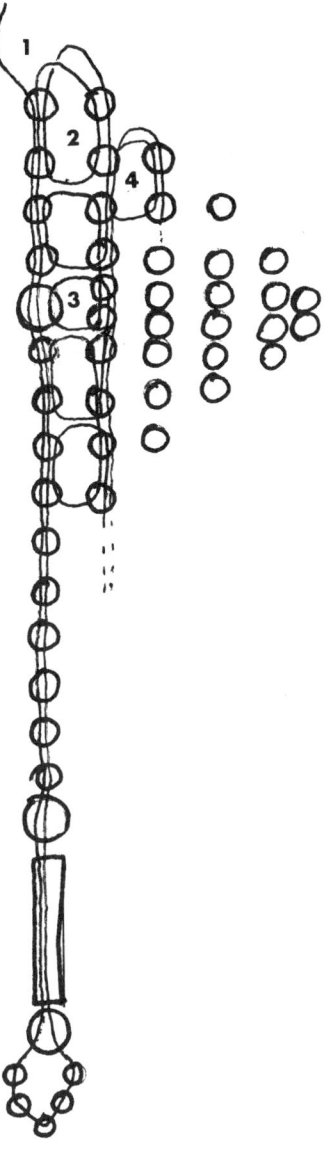

Figure 14

fourth, fifth and sixth rows in the same manner, deleting two foundation beads (one at the top and one at the bottom) in each successive row.

Step 4: Weave the thread through the earring to the top of the middle row and repeat steps 1 through 3 to bead the second half of the earring. When the body of the earring is complete, weave the thread back to the three center beads at the top of the earring and add the ear wire attachment loop as in step 11 on page 9. Finish the earrings as described in step 12 (page 9).

Triangular Post Earrings

This earring (Pattern 71) is a variation of the bugle bead foundation with a double-beaded top. It has no dangles and is ideal for use with post findings.

As with the loop dangle earrings, complete the foundation row first (step 1 on page 51). Bead the bottom portion of the earring first, as if it were the top, following steps 7 through 10 on pages 8-9. Use two seed beads wherever a single seed bead is called for in the directions. Use the two beads as if they were one; they will sit on top of one another and each row will be two beads high instead of one bead high. The last row will consist of two sets of two beads.

In this variation, it is especially important to use beads of uniform size, so that each row will lay neatly on top of the previous row. For the same reason, be sure to keep a steady tension on the thread throughout the beading process.

Weave the thread back down through the earring to the first bugle bead in the foundation row. Turn the earring over so that the bugle beads are at the top, then bead two rows of single seed beads above the bugle beads. Follow steps 7 through 10 on pages 8-9. Finish the earring by weaving the thread down through several beads in the earring and cutting off the excess.

Glue the pads of the post findings to the center of the bugle beads on the backs of the earrings. Any of the brands of craft glue made for this type of work can be used (read the label). If an attachment loop is desired, simply add one to the center of the top row of single seed beads.

MISCELLANEOUS EARRING STYLES

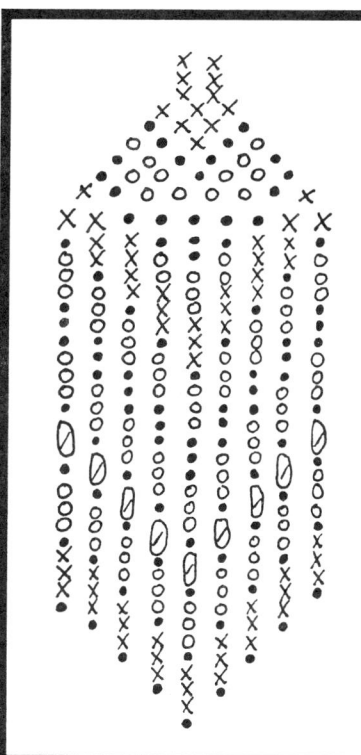

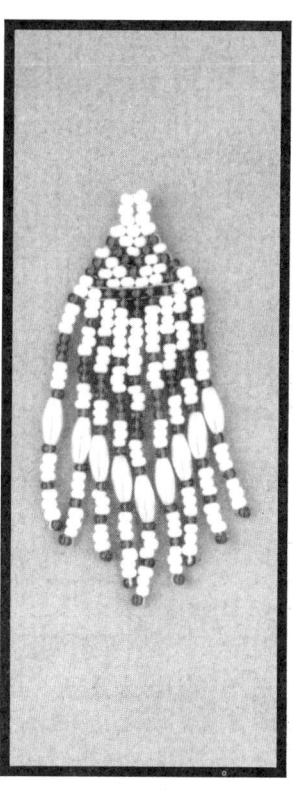

Pattern 65

- X White
- ○ Pink
- ● Blue
- ⌀ 1mm Pearl Rice Bead

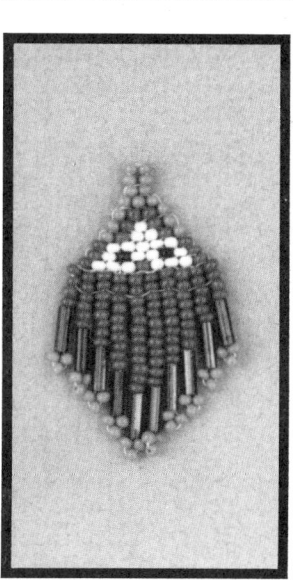

Pattern 66
(Elf)

- | #3 Green Bugle
- X Red
- ● Pink
- ○ Black
- — Green

MISCELLANEOUS EARRING STYLES

**Pattern 67
(Santa)**

| #2 White Bugle
X   White
●   Pink
○   Black
—   Red

**Pattern 68
(Flag #1)**

X   White
●   Red
V   Blue
○   Yellow

MISCELLANEOUS EARRING STYLES

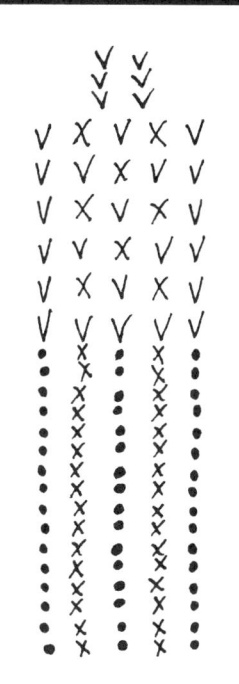

Pattern 69
(Flag #2)

X   White
●   Red
V   Blue

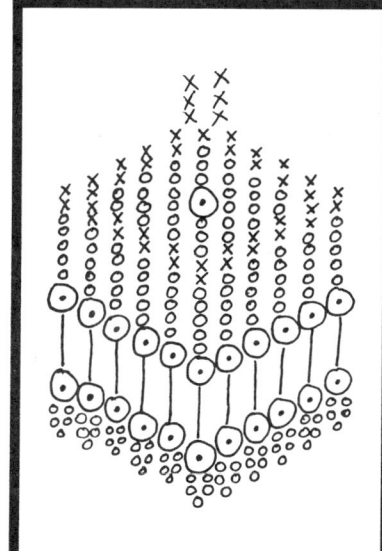

Pattern 70
(Eye)

| 7/8" Black Bugle

X   Black
○   White
⊙   2mm Silver Ball

MISCELLANEOUS EARRING STYLES

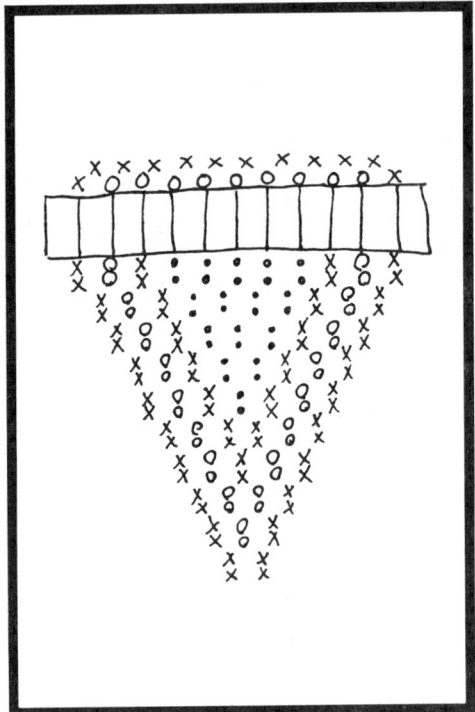

Pattern 71
(Triangle)

▢ #2 Black Bugle
X Black
○ White
● Turquoise

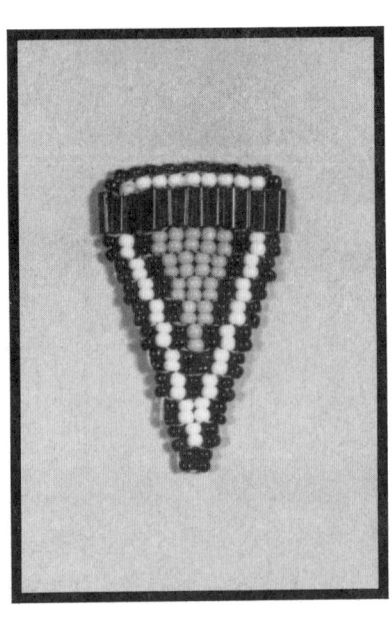

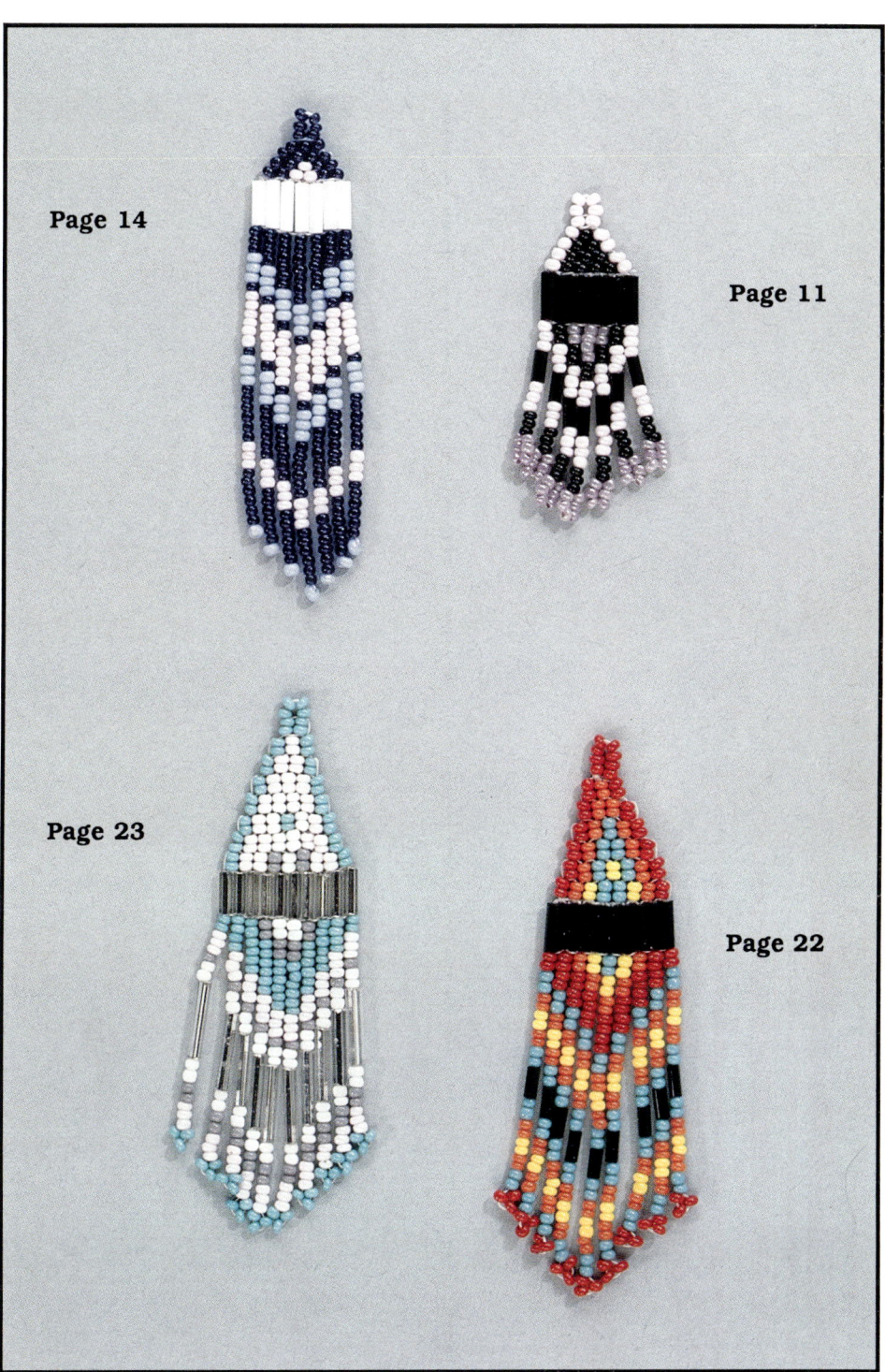

PLATE I

PLATE II

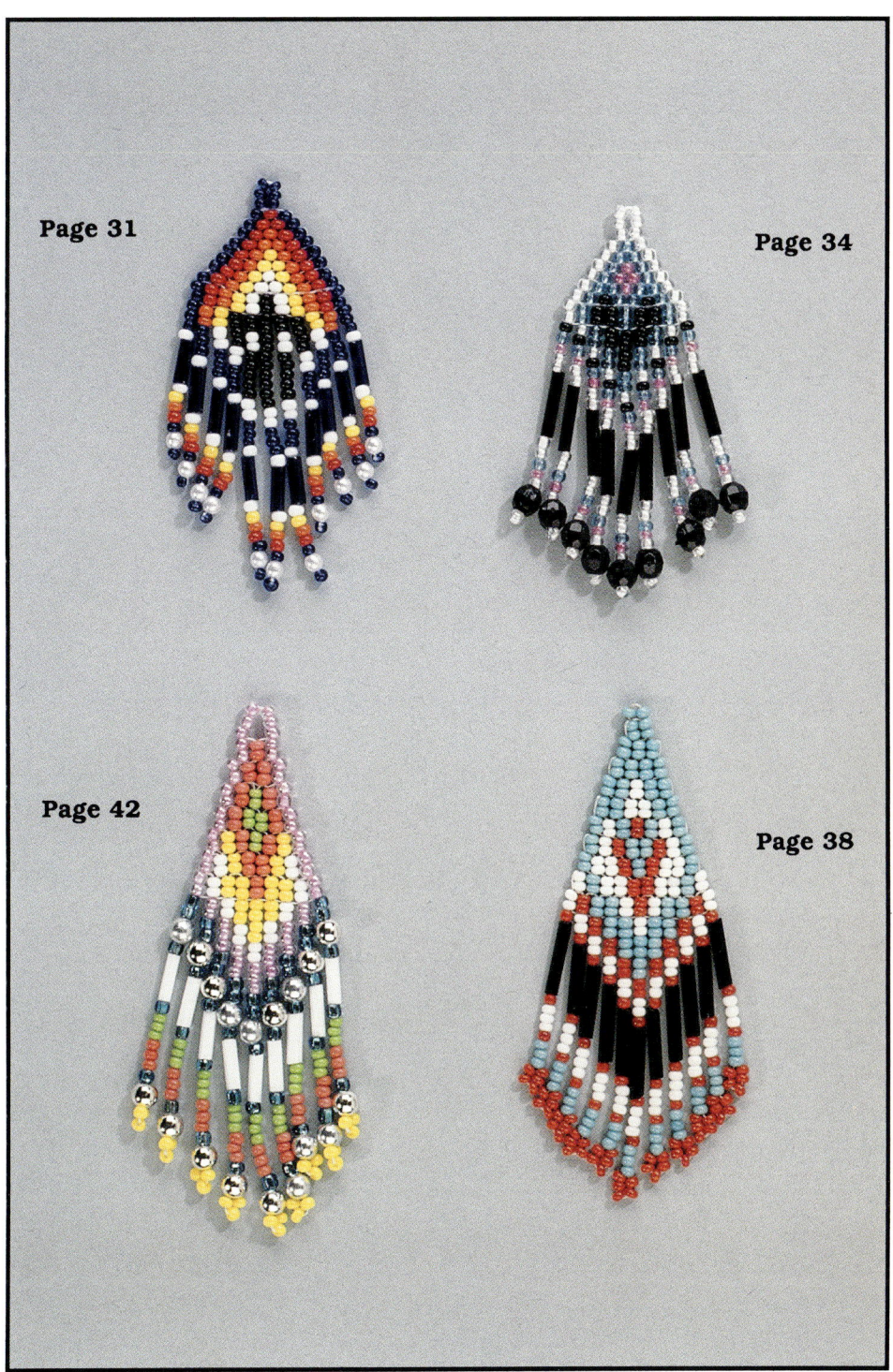

PLATE III

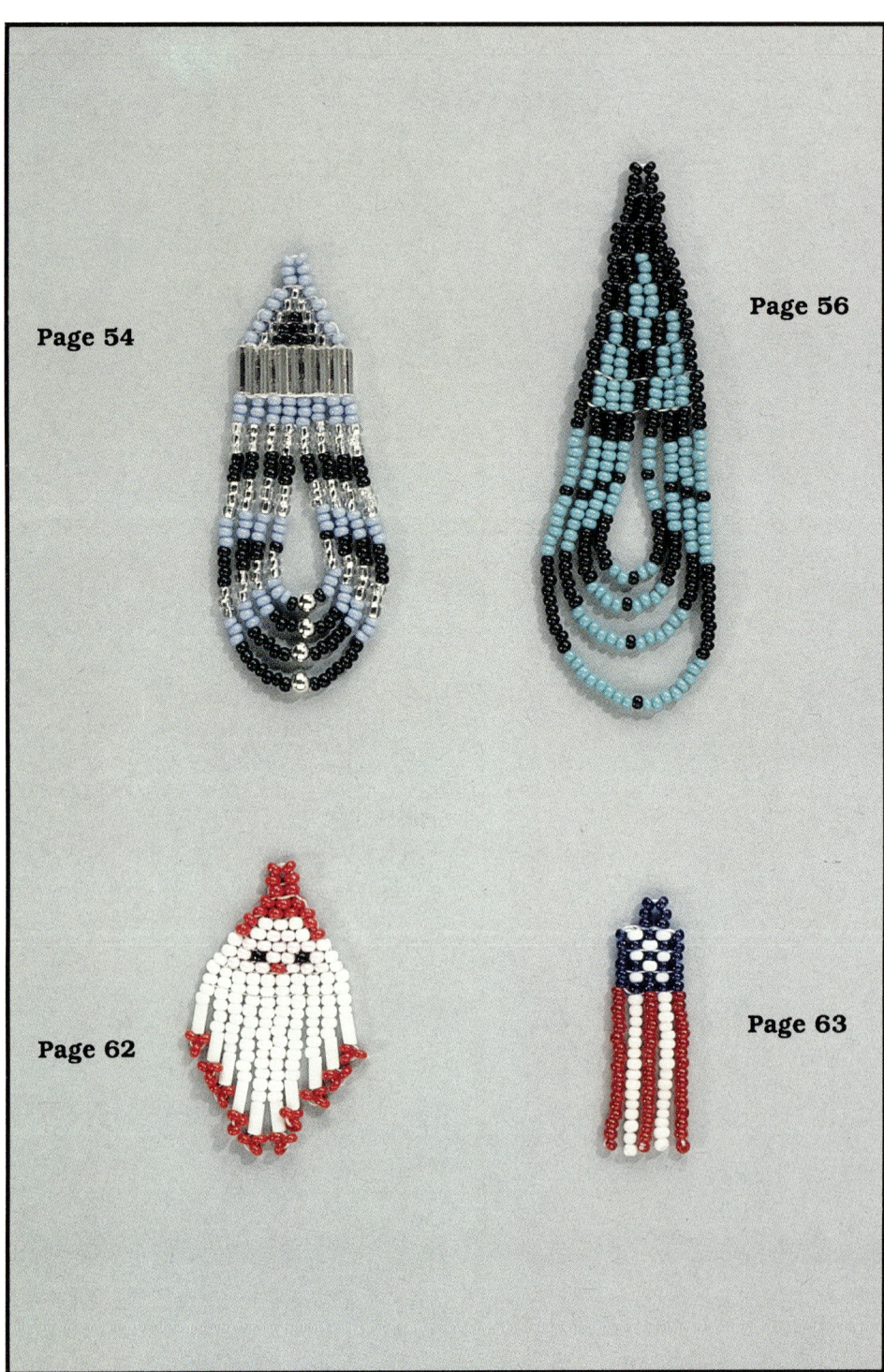

Plate IV

EARRINGS WITH PORCUPINE QUILLS OR LONG BUGLE BEADS IN THE DANGLES

A long, slim look can be added to beaded earrings by using porcupine quills or long (7/8 or 1 inch) bugle beads in the dangles. A number of examples are provided in the patterns in this section, but these items can be used with any of the earrings in this book.

Patterns for several different earring styles are presented in this section; they are grouped by style and labelled. Choose a pattern, then go to the directions for that section and read them before constructing the earring.

To prepare porcupine quills for use in earrings, they must first be washed. Handle the quills carefully as the barbed ends are quite sharp and can be dangerous. Gently agitate the quills in warm, soapy water, then lay them out to dry on an absorbent surface such as a paper towel.

Clip off both dark ends of the quills. These must be cut far enough back so that a needle will pass through without splitting the quill. Some of the dark color may be left as an accent if desired, but the quills must be shorter than a beading needle in order to be strung.

Run a pin down through the center of the quill (lengthwise) to form a track for the needle and thread to follow when the quill is strung. Once this is done, the quills can be used just like any other bead in the dangles.

To protect the quills from splitting and breaking, they can be painted with clear fingernail polish after the earring is completed. This also gives the quills a glossy finish.

BUGLE BEAD FOUNDATIONS WITH SINGLE-BEADED TOPS

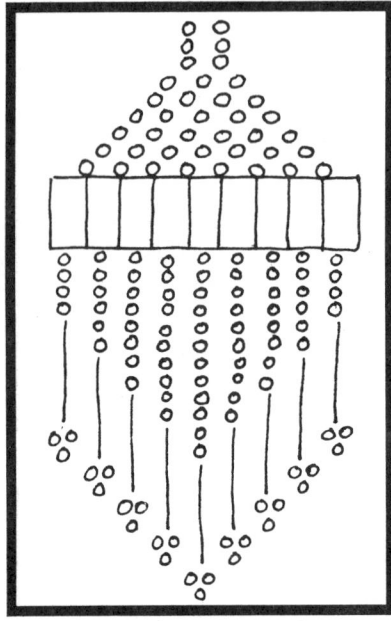

Pattern 72

- ▢ #3 Black Bugle
- | 1" Black Bugle
- ○ Bronze

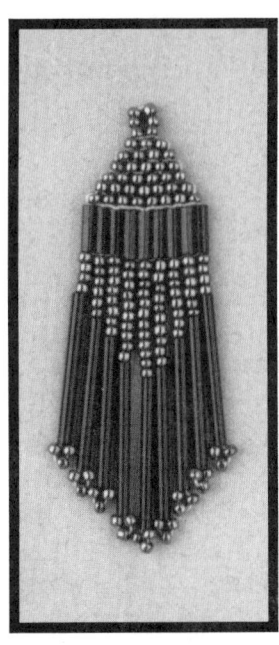

Pattern 73

- ▢ #5 Blue Bugle
- | 1-1/4" Quill
- ○ Orange
- ● Red
- X Blue
- △ Yellow
- — White

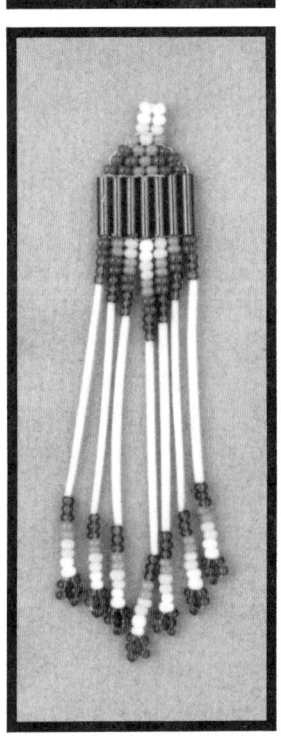

BUGLE BEAD FOUNDATIONS WITH DOUBLE-BEADED TOPS

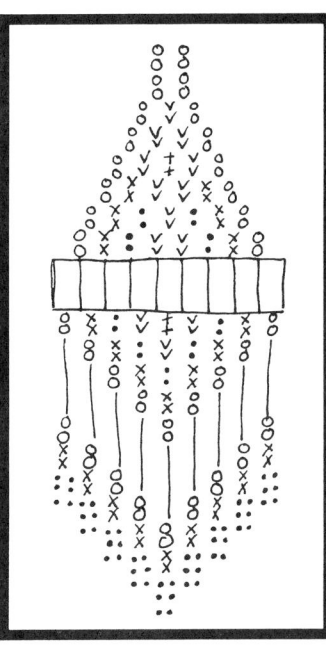

Pattern 74

- ☐ #3 Black Bugle
- | 7/8" Black Bugle
- ○ Lavender
- ● Pink Pearl
- X Crystal/lined White
- V Teal
- + White

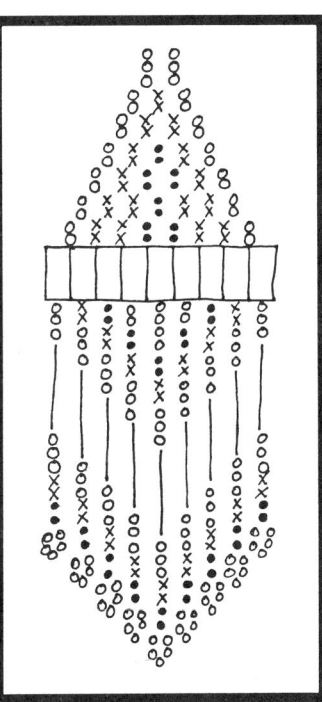

Pattern 75

- ☐ #3 Black Bugle
- | 1" Black Bugle
- ○ Trans Teal
- ● Ivory
- X Crystal/lined Red

DOUBLE SEED BEAD FOUNDATIONS W/SINGLE BEAD TOPS

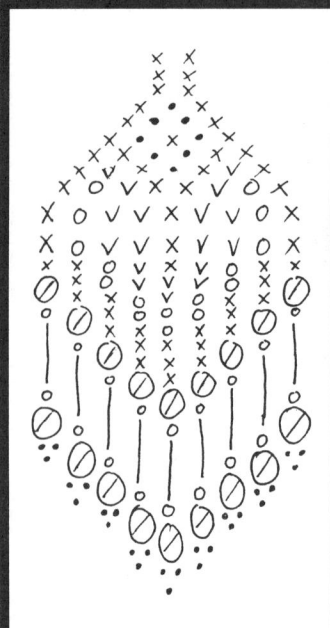

Pattern 76

| 1" Black Bugle
○ Crystal/lined Pink
X Black
● Green
V Trans Red
⊘ 3mm Silver Ball

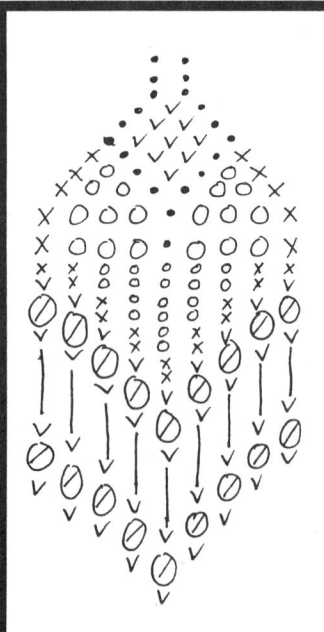

Pattern 77

| 1" Black Bugle
● Black
X Trans Turquoise
○ White
V Trans Red
⊘ 3mm Silver Ball

DOUBLE SEED BEAD FOUNDATIONS W/DOUBLE BEAD TOPS

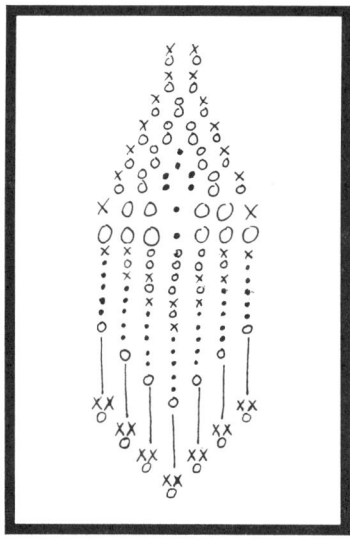

Pattern 78

| 1" Red Bugle
○ White
X Red
● Trans Blue

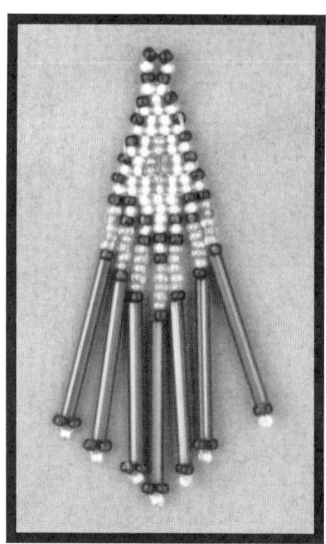

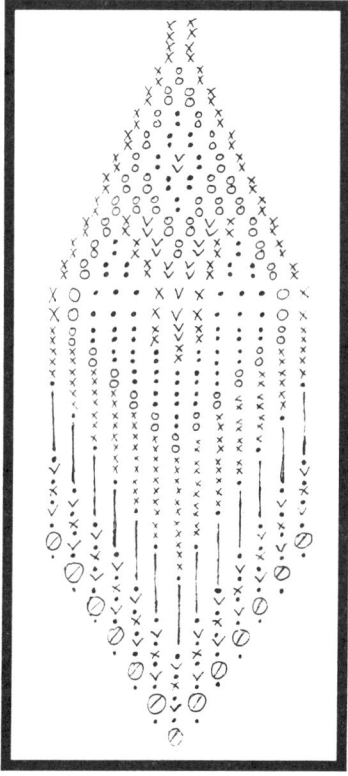

Pattern 79

| #5 Black Bugle
● Crystal/lined Pink
X Ivory
○ Black
V Trans Teal
⊘ 3mm Black Facetted

TRIPLE SEED BEAD FOUNDATIONS W/TRIPLE BEAD TOPS

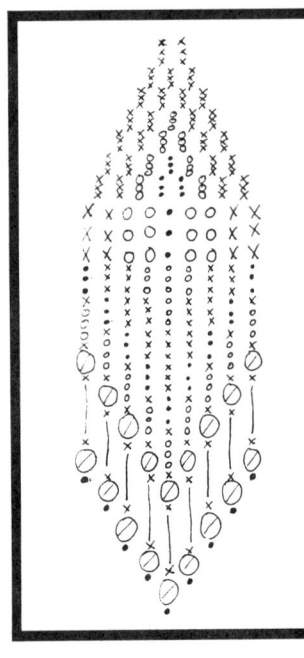

Pattern 80

| 7/8" Black Bugle

X Black
● Blue
○ White
⊘ 3mm Silver Ball

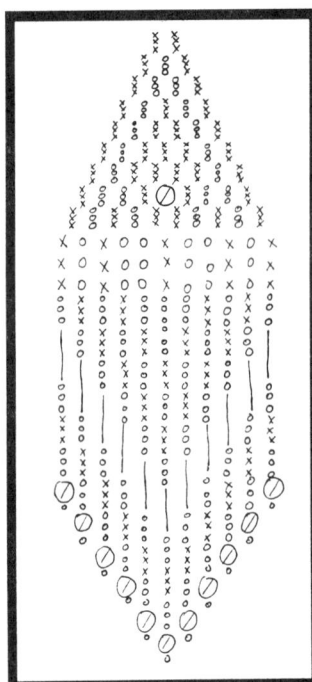

Pattern 81

| 7/8" Black Bugle

X Black
○ Silver
⊘ 3mm Silver Ball

SOME EAGLE'S VIEW PUBLISHING BEST SELLERS THAT MAY BE OF INTEREST:

The Technique of Porcupine Quill Decoration Among the Indians of North America by William C. Orchard (B00/01)	$8.95
In Hardback (B99/01)	$15.95
The Technique of North American Indian Beadwork by Monte Smith (B00/02)	$10.95
In Hardback (B99/02)	$15.95
Techniques of Beading Earrings by Deon DeLange (B00/03)	$7.95
More Techniques of Beading Earrings by Deon DeLange (B00/04)	$8.95
America's *First* First World War: The French and Indian War by Tim Todish (B00/05)	$8.95
Crow Indian Beadwork by Wildschut & Ewers (B00/06)	$8.95
New Adventures in Beading Earrings by Laura Reid (B00/07)	$8.95
North American Indian Burial Customs by Dr. H. C. Yarrow (B00/09)	$9.95
Traditional Indian Crafts by Monte Smith (B00/10)	$8.95
Traditional Indian Bead and Leather Crafts by M. Smith & M. VanSickle (B00/11)	$9.95
Indian Clothing of the Great Lakes: 1740-1840 by Sheryl Hartman (B00/12)	$10.95
In Hardback (B99/12)	$15.95
Shinin' Trails: A Possibles Bag of Fur Trade Trivia by John Legg (B00/13)	$7.95
Adventures in Creating Earrings by Laura Reid (B00/14)	$9.95
A Circle of Power by William Higbie (B00/15)	$7.95
In Hardback (B99/15)	$13.95
Etienne Provost: Man of the Mountains by Jack Tykal (B00/16)	$9.95
In Hardback (B99/16)	$15.95

<<<<< >>>>>

SOME EAGLE'S VIEW PUBLISHING BEST SELLERS THAT MAY BE OF INTEREST:

A Quillwork Companion by Jean Heinbuch (B00/17)	$9.95
In Hardback (B99/17)	$15.95
Making Indian Bows & Arrows ... The Old Way by Doug Wallentine (B00/18)	$9.95
Making Arrows ... The Old Way by Doug Wallentine (B00/19)	$4.00
Hair of the Bear: Campfire Yarns and Stories by Eric Bye (B00/20)	$9.95
How to Tan Skins the Indian Way by Evard Gibby (B00/21)	$4.50
A Beadwork Companion by Jean Heinbuch (B00/22)	$10.95
Beads and Cabochons: Create Fashion Jewelry & Earrings by Patricia Lyman (B00/23)	$9.95
Earring Designs by Sig by Sigrid Wynne-Evans (B00/24)	$8.95
Creative Crafts by Marj by Marj Schneider (B00/25)	$9.95
Eagle's View Publishing Catalog of Books	**$1.50**

• •

At your local bookstore or use this handy ordering form:

• •

Eagle's View Readers Service, Dept DBED
6756 North Fork Road - Liberty, UT 84310

Please send me the titles listed. I am enclosing $_____
(Please add $2.00 per order to cover shipping and handling.)
Send check or money order - no cash or C.O.D.s please.

Ms./Mrs./Mr. _____

Address _____

City/State/Zip Code _____

Prices and availability subject to change without notice. Please allow three to four weeks for delivery. (DBED - 2/93)